At the Edge of the Jordan

What Waits for Us After This Life and Why It Matters

Leah Chrest

Thesan Press

Copyright © 2021 Leah Chrest
All rights reserved.
ISBN (Paperback): 978-1-7377610-4-4

Inquiries should be addressed to
Thesan Press
thesanpress@gmail.com

To my dear husband, Brett,
and to Pop and his "Old Girl",
thanks for looking out for us.
See you on the other side.

Contents

Preface	1
Prologue	3
Two-Step	4
Adrift	12
Awakening	23
Answers	34
The Heavenly City	43
Another Guide	51
Never Alone	65
Hell	70
The Mountain and the Core	77
Rescue	86
Connection	87
Mind Training	96
Love the person in front of you	104
The Future	111
The Return	117
Homesick	120
Faith	130
Miracles	138
This Side of the Jordan	144
Reading Group Guide	147
Acknowledgements	154
About the Author	155

Preface

What awaits us when we finally do "cross over the Jordan"? As a woman with an insatiable curiosity regarding all topics faith related, I was determined to find out. Nearly a decade ago, in my quest for answers, I perused a few first-hand Near-Death Experience (NDE) accounts. I initially dismissed them as wild fantasies. The differences between the accounts seemed to be irreconcilable. Disappointed, I moved on to other ventures.

In 2016, however, Dr. Jeffery Long's brilliant book *God and the Afterlife*, reinvigorated my quest. His work opened my eyes to the commonalities between the NDE accounts when seen in mass. I was motivated to return to the experiences and give them a second look. This time, with Dr. Long's guidance and perhaps a bit more maturity, I saw the central themes of love, the interconnectedness of souls, and the purposefulness of our lives popping up again and again. The differences between the accounts were as stark as ever, but I now understood that each NDE was tailored to the unique characteristics and experiences of each distinct soul. A soul transitioning from a long-term illness, for example, would need a very different welcome to heaven than a shocked car crash victim. Likewise, a soul with a flair for the artistic may experience the spiritual plane differently than one who on Earth had a more scientific bent.

I became increasingly convinced that these NDEs were not fantasies or creations of a dying brain. Rather, they were evidence of the continuation of the soul after death, the connectedness of all, and the immense love that is who we are at our core. As I studied these accounts, my fear of death disappeared, and my faith became something real and tangible—a faith that cannot be shaken. Like the apostle Thomas, I had always felt that I needed to see and touch the truth, in my case, the truth of heaven, to believe in its existence. Through reading these accounts, I felt as though I had. I soon longed to give this same gift of "touching heaven" to others.

This book is the fulfillment of that dream. It is the culmination of years of research—a compilation of hundreds of personal NDE stories. Though Aislinn's (ASH LYNN's) story is fictional, it includes those NDE elements that repeated themselves dozens of times in my reading. No real NDE that I have read includes all of the elements that follow, though a few come close and are referenced in the notes frequently. However, all foundational elements included in this narrative appeared in several, if not dozens, of the experiences I reviewed.

I chose to write this story from a Christian perspective, in large part because of my own faith background. Thus, most of what follows will fit in well with the Christian canon. Based on my reading and research, near-death experiences align well with the truth of the Gospels. However, there are a few elements of the narrative that differ from viewpoints commonly held by the Christian community. I could not in good conscience exclude them, as highlighting the commonalities of NDE accounts was my primary objective, and I encourage inquisitive readers to refer to the notes section to investigate these differences between the revelations of NDEs and traditional Christian belief further.

The process of researching for and writing this work has transformed my life. Although I never doubted the existence of God to the extent that Aislinn does in the narrative that follows, my understanding of both our purpose here in this life and God's love for us have been radically transformed. I hope journeying with Aislinn will lead you to see life with new eyes and a renewed heart as well.

Prologue

Sometime in the hours just before dawn, a woman dreams that she wakes and begins her day, tending to some urgent task. In her dream she does not doubt that she is awake, even though certain events and experiences are eerily off. Her movements feel labored. She is stumbling about searching for her glasses, hoping to uncloud her blurry vision. The rooms and the objects within them are out of place—one room reminiscent of the living room of her childhood home, the downstairs suddenly containing more rooms than she recalled. She is anxious, frustrated, but staunchly convinced of the reality of this ill-defined, muddy existence. She continues to grope about, increasingly panicked, until the alarm abruptly draws her from her confusion. Instantly she is truly awake, vision clear, mind alert. Her new level of consciousness is so far beyond that of her dream-state. Yet, while within the dream, how could she begin to convince her dreaming self of the truth?

1

Two-Step

    The older man's pealing laughter seemed almost too large for the small family room. His strong, calloused hands guided his granddaughter gently, the fingers of his left hand entwined with those of her right, his free hand resting lightly on her waist. Though Aislinn had spent years in formal dance classes, the style of her grandfather's two-step was foreign to her. There was something more relaxed and carefree about the dance, more at home in a barn than the dance studios where she spent her formative years. As the twang of the bluegrass music vibrated through the wooden floorboards, her characteristic self-consciousness fought to consume her. Yet, she kept moving in rhythm with Pop, her eyes trained on his face. She was captivated by her grandfather's smile, his laugh, his piercing blue eyes; their steps were not perfect, but their hearts beat in synchronicity, their shared memories and emotions exchanged without words. Pop's face, weathered and worn from years working in the sun as a builder and provider for a family of eight, was at ease now. He was present with her, aware after decades of wrong turns and misguided focus that these were the moments that truly mattered. His deep peace and presence strove to balance Aislinn's ceaseless energy and drive for perfection, which were still stronger than the nascent wisdom within her.

    The dance, a demanding number with quick footwork, moved the pair in a slow circle around the room. As they turned, the edges of the objects behind them blurred together. First their gaze rested on the light oak mantle, showcasing a roughly organized array of family pictures, Christmas cards, and clumsily made children's artwork.

    They turned a bit, and the television cabinet came into view. Atop the hutch, photos of the older couple's vacations and a few miscellaneous treasures that had touched Pop's heart were displayed prominently. Aislinn treasured the times he would grow quiet and reflective before pointing out one in particular, sharing the story

At the Edge of the Jordan

behind the keepsake with deep emotion. Sometimes his eyes would dance with the joy of a happy memory, other times they were more pensive in a wistful remembrance.

Another few steps and the tall grandmother clock came into brief focus behind her partner's smiling eyes, built with love by his hands, its trim crafted with exquisite detail. Then came the object that most warmed Aislinn's heart—a prominently displayed likeness of her grandmother as a teen—a larger version of a photo Pop had kept in miniature to lift his spirits during his service in the air force.

Her heart skipped a beat as her view shifted a final time, nearly completing the circle. Her fiancée Dave's dark brown eyes shone almost as brightly as her grandfather's. For a brief instant, both the love of her fiancée and her grandfather simultaneously poured over her and she begged time to slow. Dave was a few inches shorter than Pop—five foot eight, his medium-length dark brown hair combed neatly into place. An amateur photographer, his eyes were fixed on the dancers, looking for the perfect moment to capture. He tucked a wayward lock behind his ear as he raised his camera to frame the picture perfectly.

Over the last couple of years, Dave had grown fond of these visits with Aislinn's grandfather. He enjoyed hearing the older man's stories of his youth, especially those of his service in World War II. Pop had mastered playing the fiddle during the war to earn special treatment on the ship back home, and his tales of gaming the system were quite entertaining. Dave also listened closely as the older gentleman reflected on the joys and challenges of raising six children, hoping to have a family of his own one day. What touched Dave most, however, was his gentle, wise presence. It seemed to have a calming influence on Aislinn. With him, she seemed more anchored, secure. Dave understood. He had a close bond with his grandmother that rivaled Aislinn's with Pop. Even though Grandmom and Dave shared their love of art—she was an amateur painter—what bonded Dave most to her was their common history and values. She had relocated to the east coast from Southern California with his family five years ago. Dave was glad she had decided to make the move. He held her in high respect and spent at least one afternoon every couple of weeks conversing in her living room or sharing their latest artistic endeavors, often with Aislinn by his side.

Dave watched Aislinn and Pop closely, looking for the ideal moment for his next photo. Although many photographers preferred perfectly posed images, Dave loved capturing raw emotion as life played itself out in real time. Dave saw beauty in the here and now, those moments that point to the heart of who we are. He made a mental note to have Aislinn take a few candid shots of him and Grandmom together on their next visit. Those photos would be memories they would treasure for a long time to come. Dave snapped one more, then stepped back to simply enjoy the moment, his foot tapping to the beat of the music.

The last clear, high note of the fiddle signaled the end of the tune, and Pop relaxed his grip on Aislinn's hand as they slowed to a stop.

Dave applauded loudly. "That is going to be a show-stopper at the wedding."

Pop's face reddened a bit at the compliment. "Your fiancée is a wonderful dancer."

"When it comes to ballet, yes, but you are the king of the two step," Aislinn said, slightly out of breath, mainly from exhilaration. Her 90-year-old partner seemed unfazed by the rigor of the dance practice.

"Well now, I think after a good workout like that, we could benefit from a cookie or two," Pop said. He winked at Dave, who regularly teased him about his excessive love for desserts. Aislinn secretly hoped they were chocolate chip—her favorite of her grandfather's. He always seemed to slightly char the bottoms, just enough to add to the depth of the flavor, not enough to ruin them.

Pop slowly led the way to the kitchen, the wooden floor of the hallway creaking beneath his loafers, his khaki work pants and worn flannel shirt hugging his slightly hunched form. Dave and Aislinn followed him and slid politely onto the bench built into the wall on one side of the kitchen table, calmly waiting. The rather large table had once been the gathering place of a family of eight, a family that Pop had spent decades providing for, first as a builder, then as a high school teacher. The table, just like the house and most of the furniture within, was made by his own hands. It had a humble, familiar strength, much like Pop himself.

Aislinn reached out and rested her hand on Dave's knee, wordlessly expressing her gratitude for this gift of time with her grandfather. Dave smiled at Aislinn, noticing the way the beads of

At the Edge of the Jordan

sweat caused her face to glow, adding to her natural beauty. He then showed her his favorite picture from the dance, one with both Aislinn and Pop's heads tilted slightly back in shared laughter. Aislinn nodded appreciatively then quickly scanned through the remainder, amazed at how each photo captured a different facet of her relationship to her grandfather. Though she agreed with Dave's favorite, another caught her eye. It was early on in the dance and Pop was looking intently at Aislinn, physically guiding her with his hands and verbally marking the time. Aislinn's expression was almost comical, a mix of concentrated effort and amusement at her own clumsy steps. Aislinn's stomach growled audibly, and she looked up from the camera, eager for the promised dessert.

Pop was slowly walking to the sink to clean his hands. He washed deliberately, mindfully. His movements seemed to be a calmer, more thoughtful, appreciative washing than the usual hasty rinsing away of germs, reminiscent of the ritual handwashing common in the liturgies of many Catholic churches. He then removed the towel from its holder and slowly, calmly dried his hands. Pop's footsteps echoed through the kitchen as he moved to the cabinet to retrieve the plates. The photos long forgotten, Aislinn and Dave both sat mesmerized by the man's almost holy movements. Pop removed the plates from the upper shelf one at a time, placing each on the counter with a gentle "clink", then shuffled meaningfully to the orange cookie container. As his large hand gripped the top, he turned to Aislinn and Dave, his eyes wide and a grin gracing his face. "Chocolate chip...I just made a batch yesterday when I heard you'd be by."

Dave smiled and Aislinn felt her mouth begin to water. The canister opened one click at a time, the sound reverberating through the room, like the pop of a cork on a well-aged bottle of wine, a promise of the good times to come. Again, his footsteps sounded as he shuffled back over to the plates, open container in hand, and carefully selected two cookies for each of them. Aislinn became increasingly less hypnotized by his mindful movements and more impatient at the wait. It had been only two or three minutes but had felt like longer. She struggled with the agonizingly slow pace, her understanding of the value of mindful, purposeful living overshadowed by her jittery mind and impatient spirit.

"We can't have cookies without milk now, can we?" Pop asked.

Aislinn couldn't help but laugh. She loved her grandfather dearly; the care and love he put into preparing a simple snack a reflection of the heart and effort he devoted to building the houses of his younger days. But as he made the slow walk to the refrigerator, she struggled to stay focused. Dave easily settled in, still mesmerized by Pop's movements, the creaks of the old house and the smells of the kitchen a form of living poetry. Meanwhile, her mind flitted to the growing laundry list of wedding to-dos.

The top of the milk carton made a sharp "popping" noise as Pop readied to pour the milk into the now prepared glasses. Aislinn was dimly aware of the sound of the white liquid hitting the bottom of each glass. Her mind was running through the options for wedding favors...Wine glasses? Homemade soaps? Small flower arrangements? Unable to make a clear decision, her focus jumped to the florist, whom Dave had planned on calling today. She had asked for a final decision on the men's boutonnieres and Dave had simply closed his eyes and pointed to something at random in the catalog that may or may not have matched the tuxes. She didn't care much what he picked but knew that one of them did need to make the call.

The sound of the glasses being set on the table snapped her back to the present. Pop smiled and slowly lowered himself into the wooden chair, which creaked slightly under his weight. He picked up one of the more than slightly browned specimens on his plate and eyed it carefully. "Perfectly done!" he complimented himself, popping a quarter of the dessert into his mouth, crumbs cascading down to the plate below. Aislinn took a bite. The cookies were worth the wait. The next minute or two were silent as the three of them enjoyed the snack. Aislinn glanced over at Dave and giggled. His milk to cookie consumption ratio indicated that the cookies were just a bit overdone for his taste.

"When did you learn to two-step?" Dave asked Pop, eager to take a pause from eating.

"Before the war." Pop took a swig of milk before continuing. "Aislinn's grandmother and I made it to the square dances every Saturday night at the old barn."

Aislinn's grandmother had been Pop's high school sweetheart. He spoke of her affectionately, reminiscing about how captivated he had been by her in their courting days. As he explained the ins and outs of the various types of dances at the barn, Pop was animated, speaking with his hands and even rising slightly from his chair to demonstrate the moves. He then quieted and became more serious though as he expressed his frustration at being forced to dance with everyone but his gal. A tear welled up in Aislinn's eye. She still mourned the loss of Grandma, who had passed two years prior. Dave saw the emotion rising up within her. He had choked down both cookies at this point and thought it prudent to politely excuse himself.

"Those cookies gave me just enough energy to tackle the insanity that are nuptial floral arrangements...I'll leave you two to visit." He nodded to Pop politely then looked his fiancée in the eye to ensure that his message was delivered clearly. "Aislinn, take as long as you need."

A few seconds later, the screen door closed with a snap behind him.

The silence in the kitchen was more than Aislinn could bear. She tried to shove her emotions back down, the lump heavy in her throat. She toyed with the fringe of the placemat and tried to make light conversation.

"I guess you didn't have to deal with pew decorations, boutonnieres, and the like when you and Grandma were married?"

Pop leaned back and looked off to his right, brow slightly furrowed. "I suppose the Old Girl must have done something—she at least had a bouquet."

Aislinn loved his nickname for her grandmother—one that he used affectionately, even in their younger years.

Pop continued, "I was left in the dark when it came to the nuts and bolts of the planning. It probably wasn't quite as involved back then as it is now-a-days. Still, I wouldn't remember much about that; my focus was on the beautiful girl walking down the aisle towards me." He spoke of his late wife with joy, the lingering sadness barely visible beneath his broad smile. Cognizant of Aislinn's sadness, his expression turned more pensive, and he shifted his gaze to his granddaughter. "She'd have loved to be at the wedding, Aislinn."

Pop pretended not to notice the quickening of Aislinn's breathing as she choked back tears. He smiled compassionately at his granddaughter, his face now echoing the emotion she felt.

"But I suppose she will be there after all; they'll both be there, celebrating with us," he said.

Aislinn dropped all pretense of composure at that point and blotted her eyes with her napkin. The sound of the kitchen clock echoed in the room. Pop leaned back in the wooden chair, eyes fixed on his granddaughter. He was no stranger to suffering, nor, contrary to his current demeanor, unaware of the challenges of an anxious heart and mind. His nine decades of life experience had transformed him. Trials had only deepened the faith of his youth, and he had developed a sense of purpose and calm that were absent from his younger self. Aislinn would barely recognize the man he was when he was her age. Yet, despite the stresses of serving in World War II as a young man, he did not have to live through the intensity of the trials that his granddaughter had been weighted with in her formative years.

Aislinn's grandmother was not the only family member Aislinn had lost. Her younger sister Allie had died in a freak accident only a couple years before her grandmother passed. Allie, Aislinn's sister, had been so young—18 at the time; Aislinn had been 20. One day they were sharing their dreams and adolescent heartbreaks, the next, she was gone. The whole family had spent more than a year in mourning, but Aislinn had taken it the hardest. Eventually, as time passed, Aislinn had accepted that her sister was gone, but had never come to terms with God's role in allowing her death. Pop knew that Aislinn's good heart and morals had made it through unscathed, but suspected that her faith in God was unsteady at best.

"You talk about heaven with such certainty," Aislinn said. She struggled to reconcile the loving God of her childhood faith with the pain and suffering she had witnessed in her short life. Aislinn thought not only of herself and her sister, but of countless others whose suffering far exceeded her own. Aislinn inhaled sharply and turned to Pop, hopeful for an answer to the question that weighed so heavily on her heart.

"How can you be so sure of your faith?" she asked.

There was a moment of silence before he answered. He gazed calmly and intensely into her eyes, wishing to somehow transfer to Aislinn his certainty in what he knew to be true.

"When you've seen what I've seen, how can you not believe?"

Aislinn knew a bit of Pop's experiences. He had shared with her how he had acutely felt God's presence during difficult times, including his battle with cancer. He had even been visited by

Grandma after her passing. Aislinn had such respect for Pop, but as beautiful an answer as it was, it did little for her doubting heart.

"Maybe that's it." She sighed. "I have nothing of the experiences you do."

Pop chuckled, seeing much of his younger impatient self in his granddaughter. "I'm 90 years old. Give it time, Aislinn."

2

Adrift

A stream of moonlight cascaded through the half-open window, the curtains shifting in the cool Californian breeze. The bed was unmade and the suitcase next to it flung open, clothes tossed about wildly. Aislinn clumsily shoved her foot through one leg of the wetsuit, hopping up and down on the other as she struggled to keep her balance. Dave, already dressed in a red, long-sleeved rash guard and tight black swim shorts, leaned lazily against the wall, fingers combing through his dark hair. Aislinn's uncharacteristic lack of coordination was providing Dave with a great deal of amusement. She collapsed onto the bed as she fiddled with the elastic around the ankle and threw him a stern look.

"Dave, I've been your wife for less than a week. If you insist on waking me before the sun just to mock me, you may see a side of me that makes you second guess your decision to marry me."

Dave shifted his weight a bit, but his expression remained one of patient mirth.

"Best decision I ever made. As for the risk of some less than flattering revelations about you, Aislinn...I'll take my chances." She completed her wrestling match with the wetsuit, the surfing gear sufficiently tamed and now hugging her small frame in what she hoped was a flattering way. She shook herself from her state of irritated self-absorption to admire Dave. She didn't marry him for his appearance, but, as he stood in the moonlight, the suit and rash guard hugging his muscular frame perfectly, she thought it would have sufficed. Her desire to be close to Dave was as much a motivator for rousing herself from the warm cocoon of the bed as the prospect of catching her first wave.

Despite Aislinn's resistance to the early morning swim, she had been looking forward to her first surfing lesson from her husband. Dave's Californian upbringing made him both a practiced surfer and the perfect teacher—easy-going, carefree, calm, and level-headed. He had been determined to get her cold water phobic, Carolina beachbound self into the cooler but more energetic Southern Californian surf. It took the purchase of a full body wetsuit and an October wedding, when the water temperature was most likely to be warmest, to convince her.

The beach was empty as they made their way down the boardwalk from the condo. Dave, gracefully carrying his surfboard, shook his head as he looked at Aislinn, chuckling.

"With a bit of a smile, you'd look as stunning in that getup as you did in your wedding dress."

Aislinn grunted, but the corner of her mouth turned up a bit. As their feet dug into the rough, cool sand and she felt the grains slip between her toes, her smirk turned into a full smile. The gradually rising sun's light reflected off the tall waves. They were more than twice the height of anything she had seen growing up and far higher than what she thought she could handle. Aislinn looked up at Dave, one eyebrow raised, questioning his sanity. Dave noticed Aislinn's wide-eyed expression.

"That's just the first break. You have to get past that to get to the real stuff."

Aislinn's face shifted from concern to genuine fear.

Dave sighed and laid his board on the sand. He plopped down on it, knees jutting out at awkward angles. He gestured for his wife to sit beside him and put his arm around her to calm her nerves.

"The ocean's nothing to be afraid of; you just need to be cautious," Dave explained, dusting the sand from his calf. "You'll need to learn to read the patterns of the waves, to know when a storm is off the coast, to plan your swims around the motion of the tides. I wouldn't put you in harm's way, Aislinn."

As he spoke, two other surfers sat down beside them, said a quick hello, and began rubbing down their boards. Aislinn was visibly annoyed. It was early and there was plenty of beach for all of them. There was no need for these two to be so close.

Dave explained. "Buddy system. We all look out for each other. I told you we do it right here in So Cal."

Aislinn shoulders relaxed, and she smiled at their now welcome companions. Dave continued with his lesson. He noted the patterns in the sand that spoke to the movement of the ocean overnight, then helped Aislinn to notice the angling of the waves far out to sea, indicating a calm ocean. As he spoke, Aislinn began to trust in the safety of the ocean. Once Dave was confident that she understood some of the basics of reading the sea, he moved on to teaching her to ID various waves, categorizing them as rights, lefts, A-frames, and closeouts. His teaching was energetic and passionate. Excitement built within her, and he reacted to her increasing interest. Suddenly Dave stood up, dragging Aislinn's board over the sand so that it was stationed in front of his own. He crouched down and began what became a vibrant, entertaining show, demonstrating paddling techniques, how to stand, and how to gracefully wipe out, all from the comfort of the dry sand. Dave's descriptions were complete with physical humor and self-effacing jokes, and soon Aislinn was standing up, board in hand, ready to face whatever embarrassment was before her.

The two other surfers were waiting patiently for them, enjoying the show—out together, in together.

"Easy shories this morning. You'll be out to the proper break soon," one told Aislinn. Even though she trusted Dave, the reassurance of an unexpected stranger was comforting.

By the time the daily crowds were making their way to the beach, Aislinn had wiped out no less than a dozen times. She was hungry for more though, and it was with great reluctance that she retired to the beach for a snack and a rest.

"Swimming tired in that ocean is a recipe for disaster," Dave commented, massaging a tightening calf muscle with one hand, holding a bagel in the other.

"Surprised I still have energy?"

Dave, mouth full of bagel, hurriedly chewed and swallowed, eager to respond.

"You, having energy? No...I'm not surprised. I am a bit amazed that I'm the one forcing us to take a break--I would have thought you would be the sensible one."

Usually, Aislinn was the one to level them, to bring a sense of gravity and responsibility to situations. About two years prior, the night they first met, they were stranded in the "D" lot of a rock concert whose only exit had been blocked by a pair of wrecked SUVs who had been operated by less than sober drivers. While Aislinn and her friend were trying to come up with alternative exit plans, their blood pressure rising by the minute, Dave, two cars ahead of theirs, was roasting marshmallows on a camp stove staged in the back of his pickup. Dave held a cavalier attitude about most of what came his way. Life was a game to him, to be enjoyed. For Aislinn, it was meant to be lived carefully, with a sense of purpose. Instead of resenting him for his carefree ways, she found his relentless positivity and calm attractive. It was what, in part, held her together through the emotional storms of recent years.

Dave opted to strike a compromise between safety and satisfying Aislinn's eagerness to get back into the waves. "How about ten more minutes to rest, then one more brief session before we call it a day?" She vigorously nodded her approval. Dave was beaming; proud to be the provider of something that brought her such joy. "Alright, but then we have to stop, if for no other reason than to save ourselves for tomorrow."

Aislinn thought this through before responding, considering how to work his concern for her well-being to her advantage. "Let's wait until after the sun rises tomorrow though. You know, being tired might jeopardize my safety."

Dave was on to her. "We can do that. But if we're going to go out again tomorrow, I'll need to get a thorough backrub tonight, to maintain my strength to keep you safe."

She sighed. "Deal."

Two days later, Aislinn's feet were the only part of her not sensitive from a mild sunburn, her punishment for spending yet another full day in the sun. The cool tile floor of the hotel condo felt soothing on her feet as she stood in the bathroom, getting ready for their dinner out. The fabric of her black dress hung comfortably and loosely on her thin frame, the hem gently brushing the top of her knees. Her curly brown hair was pulled into a loose knot centered a couple inches above the nape of her neck. She took a glance at her reflection and sighed. She typically wasn't one for vanity. The beauty aisle at the pharmacy was a foreign landscape to her, replete with items that seemed like a waste of money. However, a honeymoon dinner out with Dave deserved at least a smidge of effort. Apart from her reddened complexion, she looked objectively together, almost, even by her own self-critical estimation, pretty. However, as she glanced at her neckline, it was immediately apparent that something was lacking from the ensemble.

Aislinn fumbled in the vanity drawer for her jewelry, tucked away in a small wooden box with a pewter clasp. Despite its compact size, it contained almost all the pieces she owned: a few pairs of earrings, her high school class ring, a gold bracelet that Dave had given her for their one-year dating anniversary, and a handful of necklaces.

Aislinn selected a pair of gold hoops and easily paired them with the bracelet, then moved on to the most important item—a necklace. The obvious choice was the pearl necklace Dave had presented her with as a wedding gift just a few days prior. The pearl was a beautiful pink and hung from a simple silver chain. A traditionalist, she struggled with mixing silver and gold jewelry, despite being told countless times that this rule was dated. She gently untangled the remaining chains, considering her other options.

The first was a paper-thin gold chain with a delicate cross suspended from the bottom. The cross had a tiny diamond at the center. It was strikingly simple yet beautiful. She had received the piece as a gift for her Confirmation, more than a decade earlier. She and her sister Allie had grown up members of the Lutheran church, raised on prayers at mealtimes and bed as well as weekly Sunday school. Whenever Aislinn was afraid of the shadows that clung to the walls in her bedroom at night, she took comfort in God's love for her and his protective hand. As she matured, she felt called to be a teacher, primarily to pass on God's love to the young people she would one day inspire. She wore the cross often in those days, hoping that her silent witness and character would be associated with the love of God symbolized by the simple cross.

Aislinn let the chain slip slowly through her fingers, remembering the peace that came with a life rooted in faith. A small tear slowly trickled down her cheek as she recalled the pain of losing Allie and with her the faith in the God of her younger years.

One necklace remained in the box, a small locket with two compartments. The left side held an image of Allie as a teenager. The second compartment, having for years held a picture of her own face, had been filled recently, at Dave's urging, with a picture of her grandfather. He had been, to her, a lighthouse. While many struggled to find meaning and purpose in their lives, he lived with confidence and deep, abiding peace. Despite Aislinn's conviction after Allie's passing that God was a lie, whenever she watched him, a spark of hope would ignite within her again.

Aislinn smiled through her tears as she looked at the picture she had chosen for the locket—Pop's face as he danced around the living room with her in his arms. His countenance was lit up in a huge smile and his eyes shone with joy.

Two months before their wedding, Pop's health had taken a nosedive. Aislinn became an emotional wreck, flitting between managing last minute wedding details and trying to stomach losing her beloved grandfather. She watched, heartbroken, as Pop moved unfazed and faithful through his final weeks. And then—he was gone. Her lighthouse was no more. Spiritually speaking, she was alone.

She took a deep breath and struggled to pull herself back together. Cursing under her breath, she roughly shoved the two gold chains back into the box and fumbled with the clasp on the pearl necklace. She looked at her reflection and urged herself to pull it together. Dave deserved a complete wife tonight, mismatched or not.

Dave sat on the edge of the bed, adjusting the knot of his necktie. He took a deep breath and readied himself for the evening ahead. He expected Aislinn to be out any moment, as she was not one to spend a lengthy time getting ready for anything. Dave didn't much care for women who put extensive effort into their appearance, but he could at least acknowledge that in many cases the time invested made a discernable difference. Aislinn's raw beauty, her long, dark eyelashes and the natural blush in her cheeks, was so perfect that make-up would only detract from her appearance.

A couple minutes later, he looked at his watch. She had finished her shower twenty minutes ago. If Aislinn was spending this long getting ready tonight, chances were she was struggling emotionally. He closed his eyes and did his best to center himself. He wanted to be sure he was ready to be the supportive husband Aislinn deserved. Dave knew that losing Pop was immeasurably tough on his wife, the third major death in her family in just a few years. She was strong and was pulling through well enough, but he knew that she was broken inside. He felt helpless somedays in comforting her.

Dave was more or less a stranger to grief. He had lost his grandfather when he was about ten. Since then, the only loss he had to bear was his dog Zeus, a black lab who had been a Christmas gift when he was twelve. Zeus had been his beach companion through high school and college. They would walk the Southern California beaches every morning and evening, Zeus throwing himself recklessly headlong into the waves. Zeus had adjusted in his later years to the Carolina beaches as well, probably grateful for the easier surf on his aging body. Dave lost Zeus shortly after Aislinn and his engagement. He remembered being a mess the week or two after. Yet Aislinn had been there for him, knowing exactly when to speak and when to be silent as he grieved. He wished he could do the same in return for her. He checked his watch again.

"Ready, sweetheart?" Dave's deep voice echoed from the main room. "It's probably time to get going."

In the bathroom, Aislinn wiped her red eyes gently, mindful of the sunburn, straightened the straps on her dress, and opened the door, a forced smile on her face.

"Holy cow, you're beautiful." Dave gently kissed her eyes, his silent acknowledgment of her struggle. He hoped simply letting her know that he noticed and was there for her would help her to push past her grief and focus on the moment.

He pulled back and studied her again from head to toe, then offered his arm gallantly. "Madam...our dinner awaits."

Aislinn slipped her arm through his, a genuine smile gracing her lips.

The restaurant was upscale but not lavish, the white tablecloth on their table decorated with a vase filled with a few fresh-cut flowers and a small candle to amplify the romantic feel. Dave had made sure the reservation was for a table on the back deck with a view of the ocean.

Aislinn settled in quickly, the sound of the waves in the distance calming her, the flicker of the candleflame and scent of the chrysanthemums in the vase between them adding to the relaxed ambience.

After a few moments enjoying the view, they ordered their meals. With the next several minutes to enjoy each other's company before them, Dave's mind immediately jumped to the morning's surfing session.

"You're getting quite good at reading the waves," Dave commented. "You'll be ready for a solo run soon enough." Dave was fidgeting a bit as he spoke. He was genuinely impressed by how quickly Aislinn had taken to the board those past few mornings and thrilled to share his love for the sport with her. She had needed him to shout out advice the first two days if she wanted any chance at catching a wave. Today, he had barely needed to say anything, though her rides were still short, unbalanced, and amateur at best.

"I love it," Aislinn replied, her smile wide. "Being in the ocean, dueling with nature, spending time with you...it'll be hard to go back to the real world next week."

He nodded, understanding. "Don't think about it--be here now--this is what matters, Aislinn."

She envied how he so easily let go of concerns for the future and pains of the past. She knew that Dave, unlike her, really did live in the moment. He found the simple joy in small details of the here and now.

Dave noticed she was lost in thought. As a high-school English teacher, Aislinn's mind typically drifted to her students. She took her profession very seriously and her students were on her mind often, even at unexpected times, like on their honeymoon.

"Right now—what are you thinking about?" he asked. "I'll bet you're running a lesson plan through your mind or thinking about that kid that you haven't found a way to motivate yet...what's his name?"

"James."

"See? You didn't even hesitate. I knew it!" Dave leaned back in his chair, looking slightly irked, but Aislinn knew it was mainly to prove a point. He had learned to embrace and even support her passion for her career, even at the expense of quality time together. Still, Dave wished she could break free of her constant thoughts and truly be with him more often. He knew that it was not from lack of effort or care for him, her mind and heart naturally leapt to her students. She cared deeply about them. As a result, it had taken quite a bit of convincing to get her to take leave in the middle of the school year. Aislinn had eventually okayed the wedding date, but a part of her still wasn't okay with abandoning her students mid-semester.

"I'm sorry. I just can't seem to completely let it go," Aislinn said. "After you, the students mean everything to me. I can make a difference in their lives. What I say to them, my moods, even my lesson plans...they matter. What if one or two out of one hundred students has the confidence to pursue their dreams because of their time in my classroom? I live for that."

"For someone who struggles in her belief in God, you certainly overvalue eternal impact."

Aislinn's wavering faith was no secret to Dave. Both of them grew up Christian. Unlike Aislinn, Dave was raised an Easter and Christmas Christian, his faith more cultural than anything. He claimed to believe in God, but his belief lacked conviction. Knowing his own doubts weren't that different from Aislinn's, he would sometimes tease Aislinn about her contradictory sense of purpose and unsteady faith.

"It's not eternal, Dave. But if I can give them a shot at a better life, it's worth it."

"Is it now?" Dave leaned back and crossed his arms, enjoying seeing his wife get a little riled. He was visibly amused by her unwillingness to drop the issue. Dave enjoyed Aislinn's spunkiness and would aggravate her a little just to watch her reaction. "If they live a better life just to die and get replaced by their progeny, is your work of any real significance?"

Aislinn sat up straighter and her expression became more intense. The corner of Dave's mouth raised a bit; he knew his purposeful jab had been successful.

"I can't fathom how you can spend forty hours a week in a job and not find meaning or purpose in it," Aislinn argued. "The way you talk about your insurance job, your customers are characters in a novel, or, even worse, a comedy act." Her tone softened a bit and she looked him in the eye. She spoke slowly and with purpose. "Yet you could make a difference, even there."

Dave laughed, unfazed by her criticism. He didn't have the passion for his job that Aislinn did, but he did have ethics. He had even been chastised for refusing to sell certain products to his customers that the company found profitable. His customers' best interest and his own integrity were more important than commission or high marks on a performance review.

"I treat my customers well enough; they just don't infringe on my honeymoon, or any other area of my life for that matter," Dave explained. "I enjoy my hours there, but my job is a way of earning a paycheck to enjoy the other parts of my life, and now to provide for you and our future family."

Dave was hoping the mention of their new family would direct the conversation away from what was becoming a heated argument, but Aislinn refused to let the issue drop. Aislinn's faith was hanging on by a thread, but the conviction that life had deep purpose had never really left her, a purpose that she now wondered if Dave had at all.

"You really are Christian by name only--out for the joys of life, no deeper meaning--" Aislinn paused, realizing she might be on to something. Aislinn knew Dave was a good man, but his kindness and compassion seemed more based on common decency and his bonds with those he loved, rather than a deeper purpose. Meanwhile, her motivations were rooted in something deeper, even if those foundations were in danger of collapse.

"What *do* you think happens when we die?" she asked. "Do you believe in a God?"

Dave scrunched his face up a bit, leaned forward, and looked thoughtfully out at the ocean. He was relieved that her tone had shifted from anger to curiosity.

"I suppose if there isn't a God, then, well, I would have enjoyed my life. And if there is a God, then I'll be pleasantly surprised when I reach heaven."

"If you reach heaven," Aislinn corrected him.

"Sounds like you're pretty convinced heaven exists, after all," Dave teased.

She was suddenly struck dumb. Though her instinctual response didn't prove anything, she realized that maybe her faith was still stronger and more deeply embedded in her than she had believed.

Dave eventually broke the silence, reinforcing her line of thinking. "Being angry with God is still a form of belief. Deep down, you still want to believe he's there."

Aislinn found the thought comforting. Although she was constantly at war in her mind over the viability of a creator, her soul never let go of belief, and, at least in part, lived in light of that unspoken faith.

"It gives life meaning," she said. "I can't imagine living thinking this is all there is."

Aislinn considered what Dave had said. She had never considered what being nothing more than culturally Christian might mean for his sense of purpose. "Do you really live with the assumption that you fade into nothingness when you die?"

"I'm satisfied with the experiences of this life, with the simple pleasures and loving my family and friends. That's enough."

She didn't buy this. "What about when you're old? Will it be so easy, do you think?"

"Remember," Dave said. "I'm not ruling God out. Maybe I'll change my mind, or, should I say, He will change my mind before I become a handsome 80 something."

Aislinn gave a half-suppressed laugh at the thought. Dave continued, this time a little more seriously, "But, if not, I'll have lived a good life, enjoying the pleasures of this world and loving those close to me. I'll live in gratitude for that and pass on to oblivion knowing I lived my life well, meaningless or not."

The server came then with the main course, a perfectly seared ribeye with a side of potatoes for Dave, a fresh cut of some local fish, apparently a delicacy, over rice for Aislinn. She was ravenous after a full day of exercise and soon was eating too quickly to maintain the vigor of conversation that they had maintained during the wait. She also had nothing to say in return. She respected Dave's perspective, and it seemed to work for him. More importantly, he had given her a gift in the realization that her faith was not dead. For once, she let him have the last word.

3

Awakening

The morning of the fourth day, Aislinn decided to brave the ocean on her own while Dave enjoyed sleeping in. It was a testament to how much she had taken to surfing that she willingly woke with the sun. Dave urged her to make the journey solo, with the company of other So Cal surfers of course, to enjoy the peace of the ocean and the beauty of the early morning light on the water. He had taken the sunrise shift the day before and hoped that the quiet beauty of the ocean at dawn would center Aislinn and be a comfort to her in her lingering grief.

When she reached the beach, the sun had just begun to rise over the horizon. Aislinn paused and turned her back to the ocean, surfboard in hand, to witness that perfect thirty seconds or so when the round orb of light slowly rises, its shape shifting from a crescent to a half circle, ascending with increasing speed until the entire sphere is visible. She had watched a number of sunrises over the years, and it never ceased to amaze her how slowly the sky transformed from star studded black to red, pink, and orange-streaked beauty, yet how quickly the sun made its ascent once it finally peeked over the horizon. Though Aislinn enjoyed watching the play of light and color across the sky anywhere, provided she was awake to see it, the ocean was her favorite spot for taking in the beauty of the dawn. Within minutes the sun was too bright to look at directly and she turned her focus to the water. The expanse of the ocean before her was overwhelming. She knew that some found it calming, standing before something so immense, the ocean stretching a seemingly infinite distance beyond the horizon. At that time, however, looking across the vastness of the water left her feeling lost instead, as separated from her hold on life as this shore was from its counterpart thousands of miles in the distance.

She sat down to rub down her board and wait for other surfers to join her. Two women in their late 20's were just a few minutes behind her arriving to the beach and more than willing to join her for the early morning swim.

The water was a bit cool as she dipped her toe into the surf. Aislinn paused to feel the water lap at her ankles, a sensation she enjoyed as a child and still found calming. She observed the ocean for a few minutes, watching the direction of the waves and noting the height of the swells, as Dave had instructed her. This time of the morning the beach was devoid of lifeguards, yet the waves could be intense and the currents strong. She knew extra vigilance was required and was glad to have the two other surfers in the water with her. Soon she had her bearings and felt confident. After some paddling around, she successfully "rode" her first wave of the morning. The feeling of the power of the water beneath her feet and the board responding to the shifts in her weight was exhilarating.

About a half hour into her swim, her confidence was growing. She surprised herself by catching a wave almost immediately, taking no time to ID the next perfect opportunity. However, her balance was off, and she only managed to stay on the board for a moment before wiping out. She came up laughing, imagining Dave's excitement when she relayed her accomplishments later that morning.

Aislinn waited, as was the norm, for the couple with her to ride their wave in, then headed back out past the breakers. She paddled around for a bit longer this time. Waiting for a wave was almost as enjoyable as surfing itself. There was something calming about being out in the ocean and one of the few places her mind was still. Aislinn spotted a good wave and paddled toward it, jumping on at what she hoped was the appropriate time. Her intuition misled her, however, and she fell backwards, the force of the incoming wave slamming her hard. As she struggled to regain control, the current yanked her backwards rapidly, the board's leash ripped from her ankle, the water rushing over her head. Something similar had happened before, earlier in the week, and Dave's advice was at the forefront of her mind: "Stay calm, don't fight the current—swim with it." Aislinn bobbed to the surface, took a deep breath, and did her best to relax, allowing the current to pull her along a bit. She cursed her thin frame—her lean dancer's body was dense, and even floating required effort. She looked back to the shore briefly and began to panic—she was now much further from shore than she had ever been with Dave, far out of the reach of the other surfers, whose small faces in the distance revealed their terror and uncertainty over how to help. The turbulent ocean was too much for Aislinn and her arms quickly tired from her panicked attempts to stay afloat. One particularly forceful wave pummeled her while she was gasping for air and water filled her lungs. Her vision began to darken and fill with spots. Her former confidence in her swimming skills vanished and she came face-to-face with the very real possibility that she might never return to shore. Her thoughts went to Dave—barely married and to be a widower. She saw his face clearly in her mind's eye. But her last thought, despite her years of struggling with her faith, was to reach out to God. "Help me!" she prayed, wordlessly. As her heart continued to cry out for help, she felt her body relax without her willing it. There was no hope for her now. "This is it," she thought. "This is the end."[1]

Death itself was free from pain and fear. Aislinn had always feared drowning, imagining the intense burning of oxygen-starved lungs, panic, and physical strain that she expected would accompany such an end. As a young child, she would hold her breath while her family drove through a tunnel, challenging Allie to see who could keep from taking their next breath before coming up on the far side. She remembered the burning in her chest, the pain in her head, the tingling in her extremities, and the overarching panicked feeling as she struggled through the last few seconds of the challenge, determined to outlast her sister. After these experiences, she would imagine how horrible it would be to not be able to breathe, to die drowning. Moments before her death though, instead of terror and pain, she experienced calm surrender and a physical peace that defied logical explanation.[2]

The moment Aislinn accepted death, she felt herself being pulled out of her body. As her spirit released from the crown of her head, she heard a "plop" sound, akin to a small stone hitting the water.[3]

Aislinn remembered the Bible referring to those who had died as having "fallen asleep."[4] Instead of moving from consciousness to nothingness as she had expected, however, she moved from what she understood to be "normal" awareness to an elevated consciousness. Her vision, which had faded as death approached, returned, but now was heightened. The spectrum of colors that painted the world was broader, and the resolution of detail was crisp and defined. Though her senses were enhanced, her emotions were calmer, more peaceful. She looked down and noticed a woman's body, flailing about for a bit then growing limp. The body was being tossed about in the waves like a ragdoll. Aislinn felt no attachment to it. She turned away, disinterested in the scene below her.[5]

As she turned her attention away from the ocean below her, Aislinn realized she had been transported to somewhere far above the water. She was suspended in a vast peaceful darkness, filled with the most beautiful feeling of completion and love.[6] While a moment before her thoughts were focused on Dave and the life she was leaving behind, now they were anchored by the peace that permeated everything in this place. Here, there was nothing to fear, nothing to worry about, and nothing to tie her down. Though she was free of her physical body and the concerns and attachments that come with earthly existence, she was still a distinct being with thoughts and experiences of her own. When her awareness was confined to her body, she viewed herself as separate from others. Here, however, though she was still a unique being, she felt a sense of oneness with everything around her—a sense that she was united with the universe.

When she was young, Aislinn learned about the Holy Trinity in Sunday School. The Trinity was composed of three beings: God the Father, God the Son, and God the Holy Spirit, each with their own identity and purpose. God the Father was the creator. God the Son, Jesus, was God in human form and the author of humanity's salvation. The third member of the Trinity, the Holy Spirit, lived inside each person, guiding them to live according to God's will. Despite there being three members of the Trinity, there was only one God, a being who somehow existed in these three persons. In light of her current experience, Aislinn now understood how this duality was possible. Whether the Trinity existed was unknown to her, but the concept of both being a unique being and yet united with all now had meaning.

She simply existed in this peaceful oneness, unconcerned with where "she" was, or, for that matter, who "she" was. Time lost all meaning. She may have been in this comforting darkness for seconds or years. No words in the human language could describe this state apart from time, a state so far removed from anything experienced in the physical world. All that followed happened

At the Edge of the Jordan

seemingly all at once and took no time at all, yet, in another sense, also took years, decades even, to experience.[7] At some point, Aislinn felt a warm light behind her. Though she had no skin, she felt the sensation of warmth and turned toward it. As she did, she saw that she was no longer suspended in the comforting darkness but was standing in the middle of a vast open landscape, a few trees sprinkled throughout a rolling countryside.

This place was new, and yet, as the breathtaking scenery flooded her consciousness, the beautiful location struck her as familiar. As a teenager, her father took her camping in a wooded knoll by their home. The knoll was a densely forested hill composed of primarily deciduous trees with just enough area devoid of briars and saplings to make camp. The wooded hill was surrounded by farmland, the view from the knoll beautiful to behold. From the edge of the woods, the land fell away on three sides, allowing a person to see for miles. It was here, at this spot, that Aislinn first fell in love with nature. She fell asleep under the canopy of the trees, the stars interspersed between the foliage, contemplating her place in the grand cosmos. Her father taught her the names of the various constellations and star clusters along with their stories: Orion, the Big Dipper, and the Seven Sisters. Aislinn would imagine herself centuries earlier, before modern lights, when the patterns of the stars would lend themselves to storytelling, the heroes and heroines of legend dancing across the sky. Father and daughter would engage in passionate discussion on a variety of philosophical topics until the stars themselves appeared fuzzy, their eyes as exhausted as their minds. Overnight, a mist would settle over the rolling countryside. It had come just after sleep had overtaken their tired minds and bodies, almost as if it had laid in wait for their eyes to close. In the morning she would wake to the cooling mist, the sound of birdsong, and the sweet perfume of white dogwood blossoms in the nearby field. The knoll was a mere fifteen-minute jaunt from her comfortable bed, but in that spot, removed from the rest of the world, she found a mini-paradise. Perhaps that is why this place seemed so much like home.

As she took in the magnificent landscape, the increased clarity of her vision became even more apparent. Although on Earth she was far from blind, even her contact lenses couldn't completely remove the minor imperfections in her vision. Here, she saw with perfect clarity. The colors were more vibrant, the details more distinguished.[8] There were hues here that she had never seen. Though the landscape was quite real in the physical sense, it seemed to radiate, or perhaps even be made of energy. Aislinn remembered learning in school about the various wavelengths of light energy that included both visible light and those wavelengths that were too long or short to be perceived by the human eye, from radio waves to gamma rays. It was as if, in this place, she could take in all the wavelengths simultaneously. Not only that, but her surroundings seemed to respond to her, changing in color as her emotions shifted from awe to joy to peaceful presence.[9] As she took in the beauty of the landscape, she looked upward to find the source of the brilliant light that filled this beautiful place. To her surprise, there was no sun—the light simply existed, seeming to emanate from the field itself. She looked down at her hands and saw that they, like the field itself, gave off a beautiful light. The energy in all that was around her was also radiating from her. She began to move through the field, the feet of her light-filled body tickled by the soft, lush, green grass. Although her face was nowhere near the grass, she could taste its sweet flavor, strangely reminiscent of watermelon. The intensity of it all was overwhelming and yet perfect all at once.

Aislinn became curious about this beautiful place and began to explore further out. She noticed she was only a few dozen meters from a gently flowing stream on her left. Small, smooth pebbles lined the bottom of the stream, causing little ripples to form in the clear water. Aislinn dipped the foot of her spiritual form into the stream, feeling the ripples and the energy of the water. Little fish wove between larger rocks, allowing the current to assist them as they made their way downstream.

As she enjoyed the dance of the water along the streambed, she noticed that it was not just the colors and sights that were enhanced, but also the sounds, tastes, and smells of this place. On a warm, spring day in her body, she could only focus on one sense, or one portion of her field of vision, all other senses becoming dim in the background. Her eyes would be able to zero in on the surface of a pebble on the far bank of the stream, but in the process the bird on a branch near her or the clouds drifting by in the sky to her right would become unfocused blurs in the background. If a fish were to splash in the water, her mental focus would shift to the sound and her awareness of any visual detail would fall by the wayside. But now, freed from the confines of her mortal body, her soul's ability to take in and process her environment expanded.[10]

As she watched the fish, she realized that her vision was also not limited by the physical boundaries of a body. She could "see" on all sides of her being simultaneously, taking in the field behind her and even feel and taste flowers from half a mile away without shifting her perspective or physical location.[11] Perhaps most astonishing was how quickly she absorbed the details from her new environment. It was as if she received immediate understanding regarding anything she was curious about. Though there was no being answering her questions, she seemed to know why she was in this beautiful place, and that she would not be alone here for long.[12]

She followed the stream for a bit, noting that it merged further out with a much larger river of crystal-clear water. On the other side of the river was the most beautiful city. The buildings looked as if they were made of gold, the light emanating from them illuminating them beautifully.[13] As she focused her attention on the city, she felt her body drift towards it; the thought alone sufficient to move her. However, as she drifted, her focus shifted to a small wooden bridge that crossed the stream. Her movement slowed. A figure was on the bridge, and her natural curiosity drew her body closer to investigate.[14]

A young man, about twenty-five years of age, was leaning over the railing of the bridge, facing away from her. His hair was combed over to one side, and he was dressed simply in a plaid shirt, khaki pants, and brown loafers. Aislinn felt that she knew him, although none of her young Earthly acquaintances would dress in such a style. There was something about his essence that seemed familiar. Her form drifted closer. As she neared, the man slowly turned towards her. At the sight of her, his eyes lit up and he chuckled.

"Aislinn! It's good to see you!"

With his greeting, she immediately knew who this man was—it was her grandfather, Pop. Her soul rejoiced; she drifted to him, and her spirit embraced him. She was delighted at his presence and equally amazed at his physical body. The wrinkled, weary form in which she had last seen him was replaced by one filled with vitality. She was confused as to how this was possible.[15] Although she did not speak a word, her grandfather received her question.

"There are no sick or old here," he communicated to her. Their thoughts were relayed without sound, passing from her consciousness to his and in reverse with ease.[16] Pop smiled, enjoying Aislinn's delight in the beauty of their surroundings.

"This place reminds me of the stream my brothers and I would go fishing in as kids," he said. Pop knew the knoll and surrounding countryside well, as it was part of the property that had been passed through the family for three generations. He understood why this beautiful vista would be comforting to Aislinn, much of the landscape created from the blueprint of her memories. The stream, however, was his own addition to this place of welcoming, a place that he had felt at home when he was young.

Aislinn leaned over the bridge beside him, both of them watching the fish darting among the pebbles, a crayfish poking its head out from behind a larger rock. She looked back at the younger form of her grandfather, not much older than he would have been when he would fish in just such a stream. Though seeing her grandfather here was not surprising, his youth was. She soon began comparing what she was experiencing with what she had imagined heaven to be, if that is what this place was. This wasn't what Aislinn had expected heaven to be as a child, when she still believed in its existence—no angels, fluffy white clouds, or harps. And as an adult, she supposed she hadn't given it any thought at all.

Pop heard her thoughts. "Yes, Aislinn. You are in heaven, though, in a way, you always have been." He considered his granddaughter's associations with this place and drew from her memories to explain what words alone could not.

"Heaven is more like the mist that drifted across the hilltop when you were camping here with your father. It permeates all that exists, touching and enveloping everything. Unlike the mist, however, which evaporates with the heat of the noon sun, heaven is always there—always has been—you just couldn't perceive it until you left your physical body. Heaven is more than where your soul lives after death. It is what is true—the plane on which all that is exists. Now that you have left your Earthly body, which limits what you can perceive, you can experience reality, heaven, in all its splendor."

Aislinn's brow furrowed as she tried to follow her grandfather's thinking.

"Your death was not so much a change in location as a waking up to what is always here," Pop continued. "Heaven is all there is, Aislinn, but we lose sight of that truth when we are confined to our Earthly forms."

Pop's explanation precipitated even more questions. She had conceived of a heaven entirely separate from Earth, a place where all the horrors of life on Earth would be absent. Yet Pop had indicated that heaven was "all there was," which didn't yet make sense to her. She supposed that this would be made clearer to her in time. For now, she was content in this place, which was beautiful beyond belief, exceeding all her expectations of the place she would come to after her death. All but one.

"Where are the others?" Aislinn asked. She and Pop were alone in this beautiful landscape. "Are they all in the city?" She gestured towards the golden buildings in the distance.

"Many are," Pop responded. "You will learn more about the city and meet with other souls in time, when you are ready. Be patient, Aislinn; 'heaven,' as you call it, is vaster than you are currently able to comprehend, and you have eternity to enjoy all it has to offer." He looked calmly over the stream flowing through the field. Aislinn felt as acutely as ever the contrast between his peace in the present moment and her eagerness to always be pressing forward. Though her anxiety was all but absent, the differences in their temperaments remained.

Pop also felt the contrast between their souls and understood more deeply why he was summoned here to help his granddaughter transition. Though he himself was still learning about the spiritual plane, his presence was calming to Aislinn, and she trusted him. Pop was familiar with her eagerness to learn and her tendency to be discontented with the here and now, as he too struggled with the same feelings as a young man, and even, to a lesser degree, in his own transition to the spiritual plane.

He embodied the calm needed to balance Aislinn's restless heart. Because Aislinn's soul was more at ease with him by her side, Pop was tasked with guiding her through her transition. However, Aislinn would eventually have questions that would need to be answered by someone with higher wisdom than himself; there would come a time when another teacher would replace him.

Pop lovingly drew Aislinn's focus, which still rested on the city in the distance, back to him with his voice.

"This is a beautiful place you have here, Aislinn."

She looked at her grandfather, confused. "I don't understand—why do you call it mine?"

"When souls pass over from their Earthly bodies, each arrives to the environment where they will be most comfortable. You are made in God's image, and each soul is a distinct expression of the creator. Because God treasures your individuality, each soul is welcomed in a way that honors and celebrates their uniqueness.[17] What you see when you first arrive and who you meet is tailored specifically to you. Some souls meet their guardian angels, some Jesus, others relatives who have passed before them. For your soul, I was the perfect greeter, as you associated me with the hope of something beyond your earthly existence. And this open landscape was where you would feel most at peace after your transition, for reasons I think you understand."

Aislinn's light body was smiling broadly at this. Although both Allie and Pop would both have been fitting greeters, her grandfather represented her hope in a loving creator and something beyond her Earthly life. She was young though and only had a few close relatives who had passed on. Pop, with nine decades of relationships to draw from, had far more. She wondered who greeted him.

"Who did you see when you crossed?" she asked.

"Well now, it was a bit different for me," Pop said. "It wasn't exactly a surprise that I was on my way out. I had many days to gradually make the transition, to say my goodbyes and get used to the idea of being free of my body. That last week, there were many times I would see angels, and folks who had crossed over prior to me making themselves comfortable near the foot of the hospital bed. I was halfway home long before my heart stopped beating. Your grandmother came minutes before my body's end to fetch me—I saw my body from above, then quickly turned away and found myself in the company of dozens of souls waiting to welcome me. It wasn't quite the same for you, Aislinn. Your transition came as a bit of a shock, so a gradual welcome was appropriate."[18]

Pop moved his gaze from his granddaughter's eyes to the stream below, then back again to Aislinn. His gaze was so kind, so gentle. Feeling his calming presence and the peaceful quiet of their surroundings, she realized that he was right; she needed this calm transition.

"You have not had it easy, Aislinn. There are many difficult questions you have within you. What I must show you, will, I hope, answer some of them. But to do that, we must leave this place for now."

4

Answers

Pop transported them both away from the bridge. The transition was seamless and free of stress, much like one image fading into another.[19] As the bridge slowly vanished, an empty expanse with what resembled a plain canvas spread before them. The screen was far less interesting than the vista that had calmed her when she first crossed over, but Aislinn trusted the process that so far had peacefully welcomed her home. She waited in an uncommon patient trust for what would come next. As she expressed her gentle curiosity, information quickly flowed from Pop's consciousness to hers.

"I, too, have recently made my transition and am still learning much about the spiritual plane," he said. "However, now that you are at peace here, I will do my best to answer some of the questions within your heart."

The empty canvas before her filled. She felt a bit like Ebenezer Scrooge, fully immersed in a scene from her past. Except, unlike Ebenezer, she could also feel the emotions of those in the vision before her. They were in Aislinn's bedroom, a month or so after Allie's passing. Younger Aislinn was alone on her bed, staring up at the ceiling, her sobs echoing through the room, her heart inwardly screaming at God. As she reexperienced the moment, she felt the pain wash over her again.

"Understandably, Allie moving on from the Earthly plain was hard for you." Pop's spirit reached out to her in compassion. Though he did not touch her physically, the force of his love was comforting. "It is very difficult to understand the reason for suffering when you are on Earth. Losing Allie felt like a painful burden to bear, not the catalyst for growth that God intended it to be."

Aislinn felt a rush of anger at this. The grass and flowers near her pulsed from the force of her emotion.[20] "God *caused* Allie's death?" she exclaimed.

Pop paused, forming his thoughts carefully, not wanting to further upset his granddaughter. "As I understand it, God does not desire suffering, but growth. However, suffering is often part of that growing process on Earth."

Aislinn struggled to calm herself, to reconcile her grandfather's explanation with what she intuitively knew now to be the nature of heaven and the God who created it. "Why does God have to be so indiscriminate? Aren't there better ways to grow, better challenges that don't involve cutting Allie's life short and robbing me of my closest friend?"

Pop struggled, unsure of what to share and what to hold back for now. Aislinn needed to be able to come to terms with her loss before she would be ready to move forward on the spiritual plane. However, the full answer was beyond his ability to convey.

"At the time of her passing, Allie had finished what she needed to accomplish in her lifetime on Earth," he explained. "Losing her was something you needed to experience to learn what you would not have been able to otherwise. You would not be who you are without her, or, perhaps more importantly, the experience of her passing."

Aislinn's spirit resonated with this truth, though it was still difficult to accept. Losing Allie had opened her heart more to Dave and to her students. She had become more compassionate.

"Yes, Aislinn," Pop said, acknowledging the growth she recognized in herself. "The pain of losing your sister opened your heart to care for others more deeply. You learned compassion for others amid your own personal pain."[21]

"I know this is hard to understand," he continued. "But here, in heaven, there is no pressure. We are continuously connected to God; resistance and negative emotions are rare. Loving others comes easily. We grow here in heaven, but we grow much faster on Earth, where we are pushed beyond what is comfortable. Perhaps you can see now that you gained great wisdom through this loss."

"I suppose so," Aislinn replied. She felt that he was holding something back from her but knew intuitively that there was a reason for his reluctance to share more. However, she knew Pop was right; it was easier to act from trust and compassion than from her self-centered thoughts and feelings here on the spiritual plane. Instead of pushing harder to draw that information from Pop, as she would have on Earth, she was silent, allowing his answer to be enough, at least for now.

Pop hesitated. Though Aislinn was clearly only partially satisfied, she had forgiven God. This was enough to build on. The rest of the explanation would come from her next guide. For now, he need only prepare Aislinn for what he was tasked with showing her next.

"Every human experience, whether pleasant or painful, is rich with meaning and paves the way for our souls to become more like our creator," he explained. "When I left my body, I was amazed by how much my soul developed through my experiences on Earth. You too grew from your struggles far more than you realized."

Pop looked at the blank canvas and she shifted her focus as well, a bit more ready now for what would happen next. In what equally could have been explained as months and at the same time mere seconds, she vividly re-experienced her life. In each scene, the focus was on the people, the scenery in the background incomplete, with only a few items to help identify time and location.[22] She did not simply see her life replayed but experienced it. Not every detail of her life was shown, but only those that most influenced her spiritual growth. As Pop and Aislinn experienced each scene, she felt both her own emotions and those of the people who shared those moments with her.[23]

She re-experienced her birth and felt her mother and father's overwhelming love for the tiny miracle in their arms. Their tender care and devotion filled her heart, fueling her growth in her new soul's home. She felt awe and cautiousness as she explored her new world. As her early years progressed, she saw her interactions with the new soul in their family, her little sister. She felt Baby Allie's joy in and fascination with her, mirrored by her own adoration of her sister's cute smiles and quiet giggles. The warmth of Allie's emotions flowed through Allie's small fingers, wrapped tightly around Aislinn's index finger. Being together caused a surge of happiness to well up in both of their hearts. Aislinn marveled as she felt the simultaneous emotions of their younger selves, experiencing for the first time the interconnectedness of their souls.

Pop, watching beside her, smiled kindly. "One person's joy can light up another's heart. No soul is isolated or alone, but we all grow and develop as a unit, learning from our interactions together. We can add to another's joy, or to another's suffering."

The scene changed. A few years had passed. Four-year-old Aislinn had spent the better part of an hour crafting a Mother's Day card. In the drawing, Aislinn and her mother were building a snowman family together. Despite the incongruity of the size of the stick figures, Aislinn took great pride in her artwork. Allie, green crayon in her small fist, her face contorted in deep concentration, set out to add her own creative mark to the masterpiece. Aislinn felt personally affronted and set out to remedy the situation. She lashed out in anger, shoving Allie to the ground with her open palm firmly planted on Allie's chest. In reliving the moment with Pop, Aislinn felt not only the force of her younger self's anger but also Allie's distress. She saw the tears streaming down her sister's little cheeks and also felt the hurt, confusion, and rejection that Allie felt inwardly. Reliving that moment, shame filled her. How could she so easily break down this same sweet sister with whom she had such a beautiful bond? Aislinn felt her grandfather's emotional pain at this scene, but also his comforting presence.

"You were so young, Aislinn, how could you have known?"

Aislinn turned away from the experience and saw the kindness in Pop's eyes. She had expected his face to mirror the judgment she felt for herself. She could feel Pop's sadness at the choice she had made and its impact on Allie. However, his calm, compassionate energy made it clear that he was not there to judge Aislinn.

"As you relive these moments of your life, whether with a relative, angel, or Jesus himself by your side, you are the only one who is the judge," Pop communicated. "The pain and joy that any soul naturally feels reexperiencing their lives through the eyes and hearts of others is judgment enough. This life review is to help you to learn and grow, not to punish or shame you.[24]

Pop continued. "Remember, you were learning to love on Earth—to seamlessly flow with the will of God under pressure. You were expected to make mistakes. The important part is that you learned from your missteps. When you're ready, there is much more to see."

His pure blue eyes sparkled as he directed her attention back to the scenes before her and they reentered the review of her life.

As the memories passed by, Aislinn was continually taken aback by which scenes took center stage and which seemed to be glossed over. The moments that she had been most proud of—graduations, winning her high school dance competition, or earning her teaching certification were absent altogether. But the moments when she had either shown compassion or had passed by such an opportunity—those were the focal point. Just as she was not condemned for her childhood tantrum, as the review continued, even the poor choices of her adult years were exempt from judgment. In every "bad" choice a lesson was hidden, both for her and the injured party. Nothing was without value if the inherent lesson was processed and the souls—both hers and the others involved, developed as a result. Aislinn was exposed to the effects of her choices and the joy and pain, whether small or heart-wrenching, of those affected. Feeling the effects first-hand was heart-warming when her choices blessed others but agonizing when her decisions brought suffering. She began to see the patterns and the interwoven nature of their stories, coming to terms with the long-reaching effects of her words and actions.[25]

As the scenes proceeded, one after the other in quick succession, she wondered about the reviews of those who purposely hurt hundreds in their Earthly lives. To experience the pain firsthand of every injured soul would be truly hellish. The few moments when Aislinn had acted from genuine selfishness left her trembling. She couldn't fathom the agony experienced by those whose careers were built through causing pain to others. There was indeed at least some form of justice—all must account for the choices of their lives.[26]

The last scene, her dinner with Dave from the previous night, faded and the canvas became blank once more. Aislinn considered all that she had learned from her life review. On aggregate, it was her motives and the state of her heart, not the actions themselves, that ultimately mattered. When she had been focused on the good of another instead of her own preferences or self-centered desires, she felt positive energy in the reliving of the moment as well as the warmth of emotion from her grandfather. Small actions as well as large felt oddly equivalent. Watering a thirsty plant carried as much weight as tutoring a struggling student; both were impactful because of her desire to give of herself to another.[27] Each decision made from a heart rooted in love brought her closer to who she was meant to be.

Pop heard her thoughts. "For the Lord does not see as man sees; for man looks at the outward appearance, but the Lord looks at the heart."[28]

"Walk with me, Aislinn." Pop's form turned away from the canvas and once again they were in the field. They followed one branch of the meandering stream for a bit, enjoying the gentle sound of the water as it wove its way through the rocks. As they walked, Aislinn considered the import of her life and the sum of her choices. She realized that she had brought a great deal of beauty into the world, often choosing to act in service to others or to create in herself a heart that more closely resembled that of Christ. However, she was also aware that there was an abundance of ways she fell short. This weighed on her heavily.

Pop felt Aislinn's heart and was touched by the maturity of her soul. He marveled at how much she had grown in her short life. Even in their time together on the spiritual plane, her soul had quickly caught on to all that he shared with her. His movement slowed. There was still one more understanding that he was tasked with conveying to his granddaughter. He smiled. This was one of the most powerful lessons of his own transition. He was blessed to be able to share it with Aislinn.

Pop turned to his granddaughter, his soul vibrating with joy at what he knew she would experience. "Aislinn, look at me. What do you see?"

Aislinn obeyed and fixed her eyes on her grandfather's. She was suddenly struck by the radiance of the light that appeared to emanate from his center. The light was so brilliant that in places the luminosity masked his features. On the bridge she had seen a young man in work khakis; now a brilliant light being stood before her. Aislinn recalled the story of Jesus' transfiguration in the gospels. She knew that her grandfather's brilliance must pale in comparison to Jesus', but she was a step closer now to understanding the disciples' awe at seeing their teacher transfigured.

Aislinn had always idealized her grandfather—his gentle manner, integrity, and purity of heart set a standard she had tried to measure up to. She wavered in her integrity and was often far from gentle.

Unlike Pop, she was quick to speak and slow to listen. So often she regretted her eagerness to speak her mind, when silence would have been the far more effective and compassionate choice. Silence and presence were Pop's gifts. Aislinn remembered her grandfather listening for upwards of an hour to her woes, his focus purely on her as she rambled on. He would then provide a short response from the heart that was exactly what she needed to nurture her soul and still her mind. This man was a true saint, and his heavenly aura confirmed this. Standing beside him, she felt a sliver of shame.

"You saw only one side of me, Aislinn," Pop softly responded to her silent reflections. "I was on Earth to learn, just as you were. I was far from perfect, but I grew from my mistakes and trials. The man I was at 90 was a bit closer to perfection than the man I was decades earlier. Over the course of my lifetime, I grew from my experiences and took on more of the heart of Christ. But the beauty and purity of my soul is nothing compared to the essence of souls closer to the heart of God—you will see this soon enough."[29]

Aislinn stared, still overcome by his glory. "You are so beautiful. I cannot even dream of becoming what you are, even if I were to live to be 200."

Pop reached towards her, smiling. "Aislinn, you already are."

Suddenly, Aislinn was looking at herself from her grandfather's perspective. She could barely make out her clothing for the brilliance that shone around and through her.

"I... I don't believe it," she stammered, "What did I do to deserve to look so beautiful?"

"It is not what you did, so much as who you are. You are a beloved child of God." Pop paused to let Aislinn take in what she was seeing. "Do you remember learning as a child that we are created in God's image? This is true. You have the very essence of your creator inside you. His love, wisdom, beauty, light, and creative power are *who you are*."[30]

Pop could tell his granddaughter was still struggling to believe his words. Aislinn's awareness shifted back into her light body. Pop, once again appearing as the humble workman of his youth, directed her attention to the path up ahead, where a little girl in lavender shorts and a simple white tee-shirt sat admiring the flowers, soft curls framing her face. The moment Aislinn saw the little girl, her heart overflowed with a feeling of tenderness and awe that she had yet to experience either on Earth or on the spiritual plane. She had never seen a more perfect child; everything about her held Aislinn's attention. Her eyes were fixed on the child, watching the girl's slightest movement as her soft, delicate hand gently plucked a little blue flower and drew it to her nose. Aislinn couldn't shift her gaze from this small being before her.[31]

"Who...who is she?"

"That precious child is you, Aislinn, as a little girl. What you feel for her is the smallest fraction of what your creator feels for you."[32]

Pure gratitude welled up in her heart that she was so adored by her creator. She continued to watch the little girl, still captivated by her beauty. Aislinn couldn't fathom thinking ill of this creation, a feeling previously completely foreign to her. She thought back to her life review and realized it was herself, not others, to whom she was repeatedly the cruelest, the most unloving.

Her grandfather looked on with a gentle smile, knowing that Aislinn's reflections would lead her to a deeper understanding of the value of self-compassion.[33]

Aislinn searched her heart, remembering the times when her belief in her unworthiness had tainted her relationships and decisions. Numerous moments flashed across her consciousness, but one example stood out most to her—her relationship with her high school boyfriend, Rob.

She remembered being attracted to Rob due to her own low self-worth. Rob was a talented musician. Aislinn held her own musically but was objectively not as gifted. She loved hearing Rob serenade her, whether on the guitar or the piano, his clear, strong voice making the songs come alive as he brought his passion for the music into every performance. He willingly taught her how to sing and, though overly critical in his lessons, helped her grow as a pianist. She thrived on his teaching. Rob celebrated her physical beauty, and she ate up every word and admiring glance, eager to feel about herself what he clearly saw. But for every word he spoke in admiration of her body, another was uttered that degraded her confidence in the goodness of her mind and heart. As Aislinn thought about these moments, she relived them, much as she had during the life review. This time, free of the confines of the physical world, she entered Rob's mind as well. She experienced the caustic, hateful thoughts he had towards himself, far stronger than any stabbing remark that he had thrown at her. Both Pop and Aislinn cringed as they experienced the terrible lies that Rob regularly believed about his own self-worth. She witnessed herself firing back insults of her own, a product of her own self-loathing. What a different relationship they could have had if they each had known their true worth!

In retrospect, Aislinn realized that her self-debasing thoughts were the norm over her lifetime rather than the exception. How many hundreds of self-aimed criticisms tore at her heart in a day? Her mind had been a battlefield and she had been slowly killing her soul with her own arrows. Every one of those thoughts had been a lie. She grieved at those wasted moments. If she had been rooted in the truth of her own worth instead of fear and self-loathing, what beauty could she have brought to the world?

Pop interrupted her painful reflection.

"It's very difficult to act in love, towards yourself or others, when you are away from your home. In the effort alone you have learned a great deal." He raised one eyebrow, the last statement half a question. Thinking of Dave, Aislinn realized her grandfather spoke truth. Over the years, she had become kinder towards herself. While the improvements were modest, they were enough to make a discernable difference in her relationships. As a result of their increased self-compassion, Dave and Aislinn made a concerted effort to maximize both words and thoughts that would build up the other while remaining honest. Dave had been so kind and patient with her when she struggled with Pop's passing, willing to listen to her even when he could not wrap his mind around the depth of her grief. And when he became depressed during a change of ownership in the insurance company and withdrew into himself, she was able to sit by his side and see him through his time of darkness. Aislinn's younger self would have pushed and prodded him for information, desperate to have his attention to feed the emptiness within herself. It was from a greater understanding of her own worth that her ability to support Dave had been born.

5

The Heavenly City

As Pop and Aislinn moved further along, the path near the stream ended and the thick, green grass of the field reached midway up their calves. The color and fragrance of the grass mixed with the hues and scents of the interspersed flowers and small shrubs, saturating their senses. As they walked, Aislinn's focus was gradually shifting away from her questions about the challenges of her Earthly life and towards her curiosity about this new place where she found herself. Unlike on the physical plane, the shift in her concentration did not mean a diminishing in anything else in her consciousness. She still fully took in the experience of the field, Pop's presence, and the knowledge she had absorbed in the spiritual realm. Nothing was replaced, but rather her new questions about the nature of this heaven rose to the forefront, as if bolded in her consciousness.

She was at peace in these surroundings and could have been happy and content here with the company of her grandfather indefinitely. However, she also sensed that there was more to what lie in store for her than what was in front of her. Her soul, always seeking the next opportunity or challenge, became patiently curious.

Far in the distance, across the miles of verdant green field, she saw light coming from the magnificent city she had glimpsed shortly after her transition. She was overcome by the sight; the brightness of the city would have been blinding had she perceived it with physical eyes.[34] Tendrils of wisdom and love emanated from this distant brilliance and Aislinn felt drawn to it like a fawn to its mother. She willingly gave in to her desire, flying across the miles upon miles of space between the garden and the city with Pop beside her. The field transformed into a green blur beneath them. As they were transported toward the energy's source, they rose slightly from the ground. Aislinn realized that as she traveled, she was simultaneously aware of the ever-brightening destination before her, the grass beneath, the stream behind, and her loving grandfather, easily keeping pace beside her. Pop himself had taken this journey weeks earlier, as time is measured on the physical plane. The memory of his own discovery of all the city held made him eager to share the experience with Aislinn. He smiled at his granddaughter, sharing in her delight.

As quickly as they had begun their journey, their motion slowed, and they drifted back towards the surface of the field. As they came to a stop, Aislinn's feet were inches from the edge of a wide river. She strove to cross the water to reach the city, but her form seemed to be pushed back by an unseen force that, unlike in the physical world, she felt within her light body. As much as she would wish to, she could go no farther, at least not now.[35] Despite the wall of energy that seemed to be preventing her spirit from crossing the river, her awareness was not limited to the bank. She could see the outside of the city from her physical vantage point but could also simultaneously experience what took place within it, as her consciousness was no longer limited to a physical form.

Pop's form radiated joy as he shared in his granddaughter's amazement at what lay before them. Aislinn's face brightened as her consciousness took in the plethora of buildings, many reminiscent to her of fifteenth century Romanesque architecture, illuminated by the brightness emanating from the city itself. The many structures were supported by ornate columns; beautifully decorated domes formed the ceilings. The cathedral-like palaces were composed of a crystalline material that reflected light off their surfaces, giving them the appearance of being covered in billions of multi-colored lights.[36]

The green color of organic growth covered nearly every available surface. The natural beauty integrated seamlessly with the heavenly architecture. The city teemed with life of all kinds, both plant and animal. Aislinn sensed the presence of thousands of beings similar in essence to herself as her consciousness surveyed this place, though all she saw were orbs of light. The orbs varied in luminosity. Just as higher frequency light appears brighter in color to the human eye, violet light having a higher frequency and appearing more vibrant than red, some of the orbs had a higher vibration and were visibly more energetic.[37] However, even the souls lowest in vibration emitted a level of energy and power that seemed glorious to her. She thought of the classical music that she had danced to over the years. Even lower vibrations, the deepest sounding notes, could produce music just as beautiful as the highest vibrations. She sensed the same was true of these souls.

Aislinn wordlessly communicated her interest in understanding the differing brightness of the soul orbs. Her grandfather's response flowed into her consciousness as she watched the orbs fly about the city.

"Those souls who emit a brighter light have had more experience and are a bit more like the creator than the others."

Aislinn nodded, her attention shifting to Pop.

"This does not mean that any soul is viewed as better than another," Pop explained. "You already have a sense of this from your years as a teacher. You didn't consider yourself to be better than your high school students, despite being far more skilled at literary analysis. Similarly, all souls here know they have equal value in the eyes and heart of the creator. They are also acutely aware of their dependence on one another. On Earth, a good team captain may take time from his individual training to work with a struggling player, knowing that the team as a whole will be stronger as a result. Likewise, beings on the spiritual plane prioritize the collective good of all souls over their own. They view the learning and growth of another as equally important to their own, for they know that when any soul grows from an experience, all benefit."

Aislinn understood this. There were times as an English teacher when the process of making the material accessible to her students brought the content to life for her in a new way. By giving of herself, all benefited. Even more importantly, navigating the complex dynamics of her classroom as well as relationships with individual students was a catalyst for her own emotional and spiritual growth. Teaching was just another form of learning.

Pop heard her thoughts. "Yes, Aislinn. The intellectual growth of your students was intertwined with your own development in the field. The same could be said of the growth of you and your students on the soul level. Our interconnectedness is at the heart of who we are."

Aislinn watched from afar as the souls moved about the city, some slowly, some quickly. Her attention was drawn to the buildings that the souls were flowing in and out of.

"What do the souls do here?" she asked, recognizing that their movements seemed to have purpose.

"Ah," Pop mused. "While in the city, each soul is focused on a different area of learning. The buildings are similar to what you would recognize on Earth as libraries, art and music studios, and laboratories. Just as every soul's transition to the spiritual plane is tailored to their unique nature, so too is their time in the city. Some souls prefer learning and expressing themselves through art or music, while others enjoy paging through books filled with the stories of other souls and learning from their unique tales. The laboratories are for those who seek to understand the play of energy from a more scientific approach. Many souls' growth may benefit from more than one area or means of study. I believe the term used in your college guide was 'multidisciplinary studies'. This place provides for all avenues of creative expression and learning."[38]

The patient part of Aislinn's curiosity waned. She realized that her self-restraint would come and go as she learned more about her spiritual home. She yearned to begin her time in the city. Aislinn thought her soul would prefer the library, but then her love of dance might mean she would prefer a more artistic approach. She was comforted that all the facets of herself, both her thirst for knowledge and her desire for artistic expression, would be celebrated here. As she watched the movement of the orbs, she marveled at the way that they appeared to be dancing. There was a sense of joy that came from the souls. Their learning and purpose in the city fulfilled them deeply.

Her attention next shifted to the center of the city, where a beautiful, clear river flowed.

"The river is one of my favorite parts of the city," Pop commented. "It contains the collective experiences of all creation, each individual drop of water a single experience of one soul. All together, they form this beautiful river. In a way, the river is itself the life of the city as it contains the stories of all beings here."

The light that emanated from the buildings and beings within the city reflected off the surface of the river, each droplet reflecting a slightly different hue, the river shimmering like a perfectly crafted diamond.

"Experience is the source of all knowledge," Pop continued. "As one soul grows and adds to the river, other souls can pull from that soul's life experiences and expand in wisdom and understanding. Just as you might understand a classic story completely differently as an adult than you did as an older child, souls gain something new from the river with every visit, as their souls evolve."

Aislinn marveled at how the billions of single drops within the river, each unique, could flow as a whole. The nature of this beautiful waterway reiterated to her all of creation's interconnectedness.[39] The souls who resided here deeply understood the truth of their interdependence and lived it.

Aislinn imagined what it would be like to dwell here with these beings. She remembered the story from the Bible of young Jesus sitting with the teachers of the Law in the Temple, the teachers and Jesus exchanging ideas and learning from one another. She thought perhaps that was what this place would be like, but hundreds of times better.

"Will I soon live in the city?" Aislinn asked, her patience, ever ebbing and flowing, was all but gone. She craved to join the community within these walls.

Pop knew the answer was far more complex than Aislinn was ready for and considered how best to convey to Aislinn the vastness of what lay before her, of the journeys of the soul on the spiritual plane. He understood that a complete answer was best suited for her next guide, but thought a word of introduction, especially one from a perspective as fresh as his, might be helpful.

"Remember the teachings of Paul from the Bible: God will complete the good works in you that he began on Earth.[40] You do not finish growing when you leave the physical plane. God has created many opportunities for you to continue your journey to being more like the creator. Residing in this city is one of those many opportunities. It is a place where souls of a similar level of spiritual maturity learn together and share their experiences. This is only one of many cities, each designed to nurture the souls who reside there and provide the catalyst for their continued maturation.[41] However, our journeys extend far beyond what you or I can comprehend. As I too am just beginning to understand, this is only the beginning, Aislinn. As we grow and our souls shine brighter and brighter, we will reside in parts of heaven whose beauty we cannot begin to grasp now."

Aislinn, up until now, had conceived of heaven as only the garden and the city. Her world, or at least her sense of what the spiritual plane was, had just grown at an inconceivable pace, not unlike the first moments that followed the Big Bang. Pop also had the same conception when he left his body and was just beginning to explore all that the spiritual plane offered. Souls wiser than himself were still guiding him in discernment of what the next steps in his soul's journey would be. Though he was acting as Aislinn's guide, he still felt like a tourist, with only a cursory understanding of what lay in store for either of them. Pop was like a man who could tell a fellow traveler how to get to the main attractions of a city but did not yet know the essence of the various neighborhoods. He shared Aislinn's childlike wonder at the vastness of heaven.

"Heaven holds countless opportunities to develop our souls' special gifts," Pop continued. "When our souls have reached their fullest potential, I've been told we will be co-creators with God. Our souls will become fine-tuned instruments in creation's symphony, in perfect harmony with the source of all."

Aislinn was silent. She tried to imagine what it would be like to be in complete harmony with her heavenly Father. Jesus had urged his disciples to be perfect, as God was perfect.[42] Aislinn had always struggled with this verse but understood now that the path to spiritual perfection lay before her, one that she was just beginning to explore. After resting for a time in quiet awe, she began to wonder at one element of what Pop had shared.

"What possibilities for growth exist outside of the city?" Aislinn asked.

Pop's eyes brightened and Aislinn wondered as he spoke if these might be possibilities he was considering for himself.

"You might spend a portion of your journey shadowing an angel and learning from them," he shared. "You could also take an active role in mentoring another soul on Earth. Someone wiser than me will share more about these opportunities soon enough."

"But Aislinn," he continued, purposely calming himself, measuring his excitement with his characteristic calm wisdom, "the joy is in the journey, in the growing and learning. Always looking to what is to come means never appreciating where you are. Just as believers on Earth may travel for weeks to reach Jerusalem, Mecca, or Varanasi, the pilgrimage itself is just as important as the destination. Your journey is a beautiful one and you bring joy to all of us in heaven as you become the fullest and best version of yourself.[43]

Aislinn's heart warmed at Pop's urging to be present for the journey. Every Good Friday, the Friday before Easter, she would participate in a several mile walk across her hometown to commemorate Jesus' sacrifice, beginning at a Presbyterian Church and ending at her home Lutheran Church. The walk was one of her favorite spiritual events of the year. Listening to the story of Jesus' passion and singing the hymns at the various stops quieted and centered her heart. As she walked with her sister and their friends from the church, feeling the warmth of the sun on her face and listening to the songs of the birds in the trees and the laughter of those around them, her relationships also blossomed. Despite the draw of reaching their home church and looking forward to their ice cream sundaes (Aislinn and her friends were too young to fast), it was the journey itself that Aislinn remembered most fondly. Though Aislinn longed to be a co-creator with God, or at the least, dwell in this city with these brilliant beings, she understood, if only conceptually, the value in being present in the here and now. As the road before her opened with possibilities, her perfectionist nature yearned to jump ahead, to do all she could to become like the creator. The ultimate goal seemed more alluring than the journey, and she wondered if she would be able to keep her focus on the step that was right in front of her.

Pop understood her struggle. "On Earth, when you are in a dark room and step into the light of the bright midday summer sun, does the sun bring you joy?"

Aislinn thought back to the times when she would go to a matinee with friends and exit the crowded theater through the back doors. The sun was blinding and painful.

"Not at first. In fact, the sun hurt my eyes until my pupils had time to adjust."

"But if you were to instead pass through a long hallway as you moved from the dark room to the bright sun, what then?"

"I would step into the sun, ready for the light."

"Similarly, if you were to jump to the highest levels of the spiritual plane without giving your soul the time and experiences you need to grow, you would experience pain instead of joy. You must trust the process, as must I."

Aislinn smiled, grateful for her grandfather, who understood her weaknesses and loved her unconditionally. With him by her side, his wisdom to guide her, she felt confident she could keep her heart centered on the present moment and savor the journey to come.

6

Another Guide

Pop leaned against a large rock next to the river, taking in both the breath-taking view of the heavenly city and the presence of his granddaughter. He sighed, knowing what must come next. He stood again and looked into Aislinn's eyes.

"This is where I leave you, Aislinn. There are lessons for you to learn that I am not best suited to handle." He smiled. "It won't be long until we meet again."

Pop's positive energy enveloped Aislinn. For the first time since arriving here, she felt sadness. She looked up and saw her emotions reflected in Pop's eyes. However, his sadness seemed more peaceful, even hope-filled. He understood something she had not yet learned, something that softened the sting of parting. She desired to know his secret.

"We are never apart," Pop explained. "As you will learn more fully from your next guide, it is only an illusion that any of us are truly separate from one another."

He stepped back from her and pointed at a silverish strand of light that connected them. She marveled that she had not noticed this before.[44]

"I am always with you, Aislinn." His blue eyes shone forth great love. As in all things here, her soul confirmed the truth of his words instantly.

"We are *all* with you," Pop clarified. With that, Aislinn saw numerous strands flowing from her center, and she was overcome with joy as she saw Allie and her grandmother appear to Pop's right. Dozens of other souls took shape around them, a few whom Aislinn recognized, most whom she trusted were distant relatives.

Though she felt and appreciated the comforting presence of all who gathered, she was almost entirely focused on the two women to her grandfather's right. Like Pop, her grandmother and Allie were easily recognizable but looked to be about Aislinn's age. Both had brilliant dark brown hair that fell over their shoulders in a cascade of gentle curls. Their eyes were a beautiful brown with a hint of green. The family resemblance between the three women was even more apparent here than on earth. Aislinn's heart filled to the point of overflowing with their presence. Months' worth of conversation passed between them as they reminisced over past memories. Aislinn understood that Allie and her grandmother had fulfilled what they had come to Earth to learn in their lives and were enjoying the next stage of their growth in heaven. Her soul leapt with excitement for what was to come for her in her new home and for more time with this soul family. Yet Aislinn knew she must let go for now; she was beginning to trust in the process of growth and learning here in heaven.

Her eyes held theirs. There was no rush—unlike on Earth, no parting need be hurried, no goodbye left incomplete. Time was simply not a concern. In fact, time as she knew it on Earth simply did not exist. Thus far, her "time" in heaven could have been a few minutes or weeks. The measurement and experience of time simply didn't work in the same way that it did on Earth. Just as it had been immeasurably difficult to describe the feeling of love felt in heaven, it was almost as difficult for her to describe the strange nature of time. She supposed it could be compared to those moments of deja vu— the odd feeling of having already experienced something in the past, yet it being new all at once. She seemed to both experience an event as it happened and yet also know what to expect in the next moments. Past, present, and future mixed here in a strange and beautiful way.[45]

They held each other's gaze in this timeless perfection, a lifetime of thoughts and emotion flowing between them in those moments. Her vision shifted from their gaze to the silver threads connecting them. The iridescent strands vibrated with energy. As her focus moved from the energy bond between them back to their forms, she felt fully the joy of being reunited with those who had been such an integral part of her journey on Earth. Her soul felt more complete in their presence. Yet, knowing that there was much more she needed to learn allowed her to let go.

The moment she released her emotional hold, they vanished. Aislinn was content; the silver threads that bound her to her soul family were still there, their love for her coursing through them. As she looked at the silver threads connecting her to her grandparents and sister, she reflected on the dozens of other strands as well, each joining her to other souls. She wondered which one led to her husband. As soon as the thought occurred to her, she knew the answer. The strength of their bond and something about the energy that was uniquely his made the bright, thick strand to her right stand out to her. As she focused on the strand, she realized she was able to use it to reach out to Dave emotionally. She first felt the ever-present strong love that tied them together. But she was quickly overcome by strong pulses of fear and panic that came coursing through the cord. Feeling the intensity of Dave's pain, Aislinn's heart broke for her husband. The thought of leaving Dave behind on Earth was gut-wrenching. However, leaving the peace and joy of this heaven was unthinkable, were it even possible. She struggled to send positive energy to Dave through the thread. For a moment, she felt the pain coming through the thread ease ever so slightly. Aislinn, hopeful, strove to send an even stronger wave of comfort to him. She was inexperienced however, and emotionally conflicted. Quickly the level of agony coursing through the thin cord pulsed at full strength once more. A voice broke through her confusion and pain.

"You need not fear for your husband; you will be with him again soon."

Aislinn felt a strong presence, the essence of quiet, compassionate strength and wisdom, behind her, an energy that could only come from an immensely powerful being. She turned her attention slowly to the being.

Although he looked nothing like the artistic renditions she had seen, her soul recognized the Galilean carpenter immediately. She could barely make out his form for the radiance of his being. Jesus watched her patiently, his gaze gentle, allowing her to take in his presence and the import of his words. Aislinn, surrounded by his glory, simply existed for a while, in awe of him. As she acclimated to his presence, she considered what Jesus could mean by, "You will be with him again." She wondered if this experience of heaven could somehow be nothing more than a beautiful, vivid dream. She immediately ruled this out; her awareness was even more intense than in ordinary life. Next, she considered if she was to come to Dave and comfort him in a vision. This too did not seem to match Jesus' words.

Sudden understanding sent Aislinn's heart from a state of confusion to deep despair. She realized she wasn't to stay in heaven after all. Aislinn looked into Jesus' eyes, her fear confirmed. Jesus' eyes were filled with compassion, but his gaze was steady, and, she sensed, his will unwavering. He spoke.

"I have many things to show you, Aislinn, but then, yes, you must return. There will be time enough when you leave your body for good to experience all that you long to on the spiritual plane. But you still belong on Earth. Unlike Allie and your grandparents, you still have some of your journey on the physical plane left to finish, tasks that you have not yet completed. Remember what your grandfather explained to you. Our journeys are intertwined. Others on Earth need you there to grow from their own challenges. Your husband needs you to accomplish what he came to Earth to do, as will your children."[46]

Though anguished over the thought of returning to her body, Aislinn's attention caught on the final word Jesus spoke, the rest of the message heard but pushed further back in her consciousness.

"Children?" Aislinn asked, surprised. Momentarily, her heartbreak eased as her soul remembered her earthly desire for a family.

Jesus' eyes danced. "Surely this does not surprise you? From childhood you had the desire to be a mother. You have had the knowledge that you would one day be a mother planted deep within you since before your birth."

Aislinn had indeed longed for motherhood since late childhood, treasuring time with her younger cousins, the feeling of a baby in her arms leading to a cascade of daydreams. Dave knew he had his work cut out for him holding off her baby fever until they were a bit more established, though he too longed for a family.

Jesus looked at her intently, sharing a vision of her future with Dave. She was holding a newborn in a blanket, feeling the child's tiny hand wrapped tightly around her large index finger, its small razor-sharp nails scratching her skin, its warm breath and soft snores warming her heart.

"How many children will we have?" Aislinn's curiosity and reawakened desire had her pressing for more information.

"Knowing there is joy waiting for you on Earth will make your transition back to your body easier," Jesus continued. "But the specifics are not helpful. The larger the window into your own future, the less your enjoyment and growth along the journey. Ultimately, this is what has worked for untold millions of souls and will work best for you as well."

Aislinn understood from Jesus' firm tone that no further discussion would be allowed on the matter. The details of her future were to remain a mystery. She considered what she had learned from her grandfather during her life review. Pop had explained that there were specific challenges that she had already faced that helped her to grow and, she assumed, knowing that she would be returning, predetermined trials she would face in her future. It seemed that though her response to the challenges of her Earthly life was in her hands, unlike here in heaven, on Earth she had little say in what or how she would grow. This seemed incongruous and confused her.

"You have as much say and control over what happens in your life on Earth as you do in what you experience here," Jesus explained. "Earth is a part of all that is, and the truth of what is does not change. Rest assured, Aislinn, that your Earthly life, of which you were the primary architect, is perfectly designed for your growth and ultimate good."[47]

As he finished speaking, they were transported to a room on the spiritual plane. Aislinn instantly recognized that this was from a time before her current earthly life. There were various beings in the room. Two were powerfully luminescent—not as brilliant as Jesus— but much more so than Pop or herself. She understood that these more radiant beings were angels, tasked with designing, along with herself, the framework for her upcoming life on Earth. The being she knew to be herself did not resemble her current form, but there was an essence that was distinctly her. Her former self was happily agreeing to whatever details the light beings were suggesting, giving and receiving feedback as the plan was substantiated.

Jesus helped Aislinn to understand what she was witnessing. "Your soul takes a leading role in planning your life experiences. Angels and other more evolved beings are here to assist and guide, but ultimately your life course is hand-picked by you to help you grow in the ways you feel are most important. Sometimes souls request easier tasks, not wanting to push themselves too hard on the physical plane. Others, like you, try to take on more than they are ready for."

As Aislinn watched, other beings, similar in vibration to her past self, entered the room. She recognized them despite their altered appearance. Her grandfather, grandmother, and Allie were among those present. Aislinn's former self was excitedly gesturing at the plan on the table-like surface before them. Pop, Grandma, and Allie's faces were marked with concern and confusion.

Jesus laughed. "You were determined to challenge yourself in this life. Though working through loss and grief was something that your guides agreed would be beneficial for your growth, the timeline was to be much more spread out, to give your soul time to recover."

Aislinn grimaced. "I assume I ended up getting my way."

"Yes. The souls who would be your sister and grandparents were minimally affected by your decisions and reluctantly agreed to the plan as well, despite their concern that you would incur unnecessary suffering. In the end, it was important to honor your choice."

In the room before them, her sister and grandparents exited, and a few other souls entered. Aislinn quickly recognized one as Dave. The other new souls also felt somehow familiar, but no one she could identify from the physical plane.

"The rest of your life plan is deeply intertwined with those of these souls," Jesus said. "You made them promises that you must now keep. That is why you must return."

Aislinn understood the responsibility she had to these souls but wondered about the details of what she had promised. "My death, my being here, was it also part of the plan?"

"Originally no, but the quick succession of losses was taking a greater toll on your soul than expected. You were suffering in a way that would have made it difficult for you to grow as you had hoped."

Aislinn read between the lines. "Is that why you brought me here?"

Jesus knew that Aislinn's time on the spiritual plane would also serve to bring a bit of the wisdom and heart of God back to Earth, a role that Aislinn's deep compassion for other souls would make her eager to take on. However, that would be revealed in time.

"Yes, Aislinn," Jesus answered. "That is one of the reasons you are here. Yours is a very unusual situation. This is the first time in many lifetimes that you have needed significant redirection to continue on your path."

Jesus paused, knowing this last bit of knowledge would bring more questions.

Aislinn was getting used to surprises, but this one seemed to contradict the core of her Christian faith. Coming from Jesus, however, meant that it must be true.

"Previous lifetimes...do you mean this was not my first experience on Earth?"

In answer, Jesus turned slowly; her gaze followed his. They were back in the wooded knoll, the tall maple, oak, and sycamore trees that Aislinn remembered from her childhood surrounding them. There was a new addition to the knoll, an oak bench under a large poplar tree, strategically placed by Jesus as a place to enjoy the quiet beauty of the woods. The bench looked worn from use, or perhaps age, the wear causing it to blend in naturally with the bark of the trees surrounding it. Jesus sat on the bench and indicated that she should do likewise.

Once he sensed Aislinn had settled into the vivid visual beauty and aromas of this place, he did his best to relay an answer to her question. "Yes, every soul experiences many lifetimes. A soul might experience hundreds of lifetimes on Earth alone."

Aislinn still struggled with this, as she did not remember any prior lifetimes.

"You have lived many lifetimes, and dozens on Earth," Jesus explained. "This information would have been overwhelming when you first made the transition, but it is appropriate now."

As soon as Jesus had finished speaking, the memories washed back over her. A myriad of life experiences flashed before her, ranging from ancient times to the Middle Ages and ending with her soul's most recent incarnation as a battlefield nurse for Austria in World War I. Places she had not heard about came racing back to her. She suddenly saw herself preparing clean bandages on the Italian front. News came that the Italians had attacked the Isonzo River. The days blurred together as she spent long hours at the bedsides of dozens of soldiers, struggling to keep their spirits as well as her own as positive as possible. As the memories came flooding back, she was touched by how much she had grown through her various life experiences. There was a clear trend towards greater wisdom and compassion as she progressed. Though her roles, nationalities, and characteristics varied greatly from one incarnation to the next, there was still an essence that was uniquely hers that carried throughout.[48]

Aislinn considered the implications of what she had just experienced.

"So not all people on Earth are at the same point in their soul's evolution?" she asked.

"That is correct. Some are on their first experience on Earth or may only spend a single lifetime on your planet for a very specific purpose, a purpose that only Earth can provide. Others have almost grown beyond the lessons Earth offers."

Aislinn thought of the many people, including some of her students and relatives, who seemed unable to think about anyone besides themselves. For others, a heart of service came more naturally.

"That would explain some of the more self-centered behavior on Earth," Aislinn said.

"In part. There are any number of reasons why a soul may make choices that appear to come from inexperience. Highly evolved souls may struggle with a particular lesson. Some souls, as you well know, might choose challenges or experiences that are more than what they were ready for. Finally, all souls can easily get wrapped up in the distractions of the world. A soul may become spiritually separated from God and make decisions out of ignorance, confusion, or fear."[49]

Jesus paused, desiring that what he would say next be heard clearly. He looked at Aislinn. She could feel the intensity of his gaze and the strength of his emotion.

"You must never look down on another soul, Aislinn. You too were once inexperienced on Earth. You have had lifetimes when you struggled more than expected. Regardless of where a soul is on their journey or what truth they may have forgotten, every soul has worth beyond measure in the eyes of God."[50]

Aislinn understood. Just as she had experienced in the heavenly city, all souls were meant to help each other, regardless of their level of evolution, experience, or talents. They all depended on one other, their experiences coming together to form the river of life.

"We are all interconnected—they are a part of me," Aislinn said, trying to summarize all that was running through her consciousness.

"Yes," Jesus replied. "You are all a part of each other and must help one another on your journeys. That is why I taught you to love one another as yourself[51]—you are all a part of God's creation and therefore a part of each other. When you show kindness and compassion to others, regardless of whether it is received or understood, you are giving that same gift to yourself as well."

Aislinn was beginning to understand that her interconnectedness with all beings was a core truth—one that she hoped she would be able to live from when she returned. She was comforted by the progress she had made in her many lifetimes so far on Earth. However, the thought of living out hundreds more was terrifying. She was already struggling with returning to finish out her current life.

"Does that mean I must experience many more lifetimes on Earth before I can live in the city?" she asked.

Jesus laughed. "Eternity is a concept that the human mind cannot grasp. It is yet difficult to comprehend in your adjustment to the spiritual plane, Aislinn. For now, simply rest assured that the journey before you is expansive enough for any and all that you want or need as you spiritually mature. Remember that heaven includes all that exists. In the span of eternity, you will reside in many of the cities here as well as shadow angels and serve as a guide to souls on the physical plane. Before your next lifetime, you and your guides will choose the experiences here that will most help you grow, and then work to design your next incarnation, whether on Earth or elsewhere. Because of the importance and intensity of the lessons you learn at this point in your soul's growth, the challenging environment and separation from the divine of Earth is helpful. However, your time on Earth, even the sum total of all your lifetimes there, is a small drop in the bucket of all that you will experience as you grow to be more like your creator. Every soul grows at its own pace; there is no pressure, no blame for needing to relearn lessons or for taking a lifetime simply to have fun."[52]

"Fun?" Aislinn thought, realizing that this was yet another reason why it was not helpful to judge others' progress on Earth. "That's why some people seem to have it so easy."

Jesus, hearing her thought, continued. "It's true that a few souls may take a lifetime just to experience something that only a life on your planet can offer—playing tennis for instance.[53] You should never judge another soul, Aislinn. While one soul has an easy road because he is there to enjoy an experience unique to Earth, another may be on their last lifetime on Earth and have only a few small lessons to master there. Similarly, someone who is struggling could be working through a difficult lesson, having difficulty staying on their life course, or be on Earth to help others with their lessons. In fact, some souls who choose bodies with mental or physical handicaps are beings ready for an incarnation on another planet. However, these souls choose to return to Earth in forms with disabilities to teach others through their hardships."

"So, there's no way to recognize the more highly evolved souls?" she asked, her mind thinking about a few people she knew on Earth whom she suspected had been around a bit longer than she had.

"It would be both difficult and a waste of your energy. Instead, stay focused on learning the lessons you chose for yourself. Meanwhile, do your best to honor and care for other souls and appreciate their uniqueness as you journey."

Jesus paused, reaching out to touch a wildflower growing adjacent to the bench. Aislinn loved how Jesus seemed to enjoy every intricate detail of this place as much as she did, despite his having experienced it for an eternity.

"Your Father desires your happiness," he said, brushing his hand across the petals, then gesturing towards the whole of the small forest. "He created all this for your enjoyment. Every planet, every sphere of heaven was created to demonstrate his love for you."

Aislinn's eyes widened at the thought. It stood to reason, with the vastness of heaven, that there would be life elsewhere, but until their current discussion, she had not yet considered this. Aislinn knew that here, her questions brought her answers, and her desires were satisfied. When she yearned to see the city, her body flew towards it. When she felt a question rise within her, her guide had an answer ready and waiting. With few exceptions, what she desired was granted. In this case, she felt a hint of fear, intensified by the science fiction stories of her youth. Yet, the daring of her spirit, consistent with though not due to her Irish bloodline, drove her to press on. She gave voice to her request.

"May I see these planets?"[54]

At once, as if the thought itself granted her desire, she was on another sphere, more dimly lit than the luminescent heavenly landscape, but with features, colors, and beauty far surpassing those of Earth. Instead of the one brilliant yellow sun of Earth, two light orbs lit the sky. The brighter of the two was still dim enough that Aislinn could look at it directly, though only briefly, without hurting her eyes. It glowed a beautiful red color. The second was much dimmer and radiated a pale white. She could see beautiful buildings in a nearby city that reminded her of those in the heavenly city— their exteriors seemed to be covered in crystals. The city was filled with life, animals and human-like beings moving about with a joyful energy. Aislinn drew closer to several human-like beings who were walking towards the city. These beings were tall and willowy in appearance, with beautiful, golden skin. As she approached them, they paused and turned towards her, expressions of curiosity marking their faces.

"Can you.... see me?" Aislinn asked cautiously. Her questions were relayed telepathically to them.

"Yes, but we do not recognize your kind. What planet are you from?" They spoke a language foreign to her, yet the meaning of their words was instantly clear.

Aislinn told them of Earth and was able to show them her home planet simply by bringing it into her own mental focus. The beings expressed great interest in what she showed them, her consciousness scanning the memories of her previous experiences on Earth. As Aislinn considered each memory, the beings were able to experience each memory with her. They were a polite, engaged audience, sharing her joys and expressing their curiosity through their requests for more detail about some scenes. They seemed to take pleasure in experiencing, through Aislinn, the novel experiences that Earth offered. After sharing one particular memory though, Aislinn sensed mild discomfort and even shock from her new companions. She was puzzled—the memory seemed so benign. She was reminiscing about a holiday meal with her family, complete with a perfectly roasted ham.

"I don't understand. Did I upset you?" Aislinn asked, hesitantly.

"We didn't know there were beings who consumed other life for their energy," one communicated, showing curiosity with a hint of disgust.

She was taken aback. "How do you obtain your energy here?"

"From the power of the universe directly—what you might refer to as 'God'. We do not 'eat' as you do. We simply receive all we need directly through our connection to God."

"How beautiful!" she thought. Clearly these beings were of higher evolution than most on Earth.

Aislinn motioned to the city and asked them about how the crystal buildings were constructed, her grandfather's experience in home-building sparking her curiosity.

"We grow them," one being explained. "We use our minds and energy, rather than tools and our bodies, as you do."

The beings took great joy in teaching Aislinn about their city. As they spoke with her, she realized the similarities they shared with the beings she had observed in the heavenly city. Just like the souls in the heavenly city, they thrived on caring for and teaching one another.

Aislinn thanked them for their teaching and their kindness. This planet was devoid of any of the negative emotions she felt on Earth. The beings clearly had abilities that humans did not. They communicated through telepathy, possessed an ability to work with spiritual energy, and had an awareness of and communication with beings on other planets. She looked forward to continuing her growth and living in such beautiful places herself. However, she also wondered what sort of planet would be appropriate for beings less evolved than humans.

As before, as soon as she desired to see this lower level of existence, she was instantly transported there. This world closely resembled Earth—the flora and fauna reminiscent of those from a coniferous forest. The beings here reminded her of early humans on Earth. They were rather hairy, and, unlike the beings on the first planet, they did not seem to recognize her presence. Aislinn watched them interact with one another for a time. They were gathered around a recent kill, cutting portions of meat with primitive tools and speaking in a cruder language. She quickly tired of watching the scene, unable to interact with these souls. As soon as her curiosity was satisfied, she was immediately back with Jesus in the wooded knoll.

Aislinn wondered at the huge difference in her experience on the two planets. "Why could the beings on the first planet see me, while those on the second could not?"

"Excellent observation, Aislinn." Jesus stood and began to walk along a dirt path through the trees. Naturally, Aislinn followed. "As beings evolve, they become more cognizant of other spiritual beings, even while they are in their bodily forms. Regardless of the planet, spiritual beings abound: spirits, guides, and what people on Earth call guardian angels. This is true for the planets you just visited as well. Spiritual beings were present, though, not expecting them during your visit, you did not think to look for them. Beings living on planets designed for more highly evolved souls are acutely aware of the presence of these beings and interact freely with them, as those you visited on the first planet did with you. They live in harmony with both planes—the spiritual and the material—gaining all their energy and guidance from spiritual sources."

"Is that why they reacted to the memory of the Christmas dinner?"

"Yes. They too at one point consumed other beings for food, thousands of lifetimes ago, but it is a distant memory for them and seemed shocking. Eating meat is perfectly normal and acceptable on Earth. You will remember that I prepared a breakfast of fish for my disciples?[55] But, as souls evolve, even the physical bodies they incarnate into change. You may have noticed that their bodies seemed leaner and less muscular than your own and that they relied on their minds rather than their bodies to perform labor?"

Aislinn nodded.

"The beings on that planet rely so much less on physical abilities and strength, even though they live on the physical plane. They exist in part on both planes—physical and spiritual. However, on less evolved planets, they live almost exclusively on the material plane, and are completely oblivious to our existence. On planets in-between, such as your own, incarnate beings live primarily in the material world, but catch glimpses of the true reality. As souls evolve, they move closer to their source, God. They also become more aware of the spiritual realm while in their incarnate forms."

Aislinn wondered just how much of the spiritual dimension on Earth she had been oblivious too.

Jesus smiled. "You are completely surrounded by spiritual beings while on Earth, Aislinn. Your body and mind are not designed to perceive them, though you can become more aware of the spiritual realm over time. On Earth, a person can live amongst dozens of species of birds or flowers and yet walk past them daily, completely unaware on their presence. It takes a discerning eye and ear to notice the abundance of nature but being unaware of its presence does not alter reality. In a similar way, you are surrounded by the divine, whether you are aware of it or not."

7

Never Alone

As they strolled through the small forest, Aislinn pondered how much of this spiritual reality she had been aware of on Earth, even subconsciously.

"So many times, I could have sworn I felt something—a nudge in the right direction, a loving presence, happenings that seemed too perfect to be coincidence," she said.

Jesus nodded. "Some are figments of the imagination, but most are genuine interactions with the spiritual plane. All too often, people on Earth will fail to believe in the presence of spiritual beings because it is too foreign a concept, from an Earthly perspective, to be surrounded and infused as you are by the divine. It is easier to explain the 'strange' moments away than seriously consider the reality of the spiritual realm."

Aislinn wondered just how much she had been oblivious to. Sensing her question, Jesus shifted their frame of reference to Earth. Though she couldn't pinpoint the exact location, she was aware that they were in a larger city, the buildings dozens of stories tall and the sidewalks well-traveled. The din of the city at mid-day surrounded them: truck engines, car radios, and the occasional horn from an impatient driver. They were hovering over a busy intersection where at least fifteen vehicles, in addition to several pedestrians, were visible. Gliding next to each person, unhindered by physical barriers, was a spiritual being.

"Some are angels," Jesus indicated, pointing to a bright being with indiscernible features who hovered near the left shoulder of a stout, middle-aged man waiting to cross the street. "Others are relatives who had completed their incarnation prior to the birth of the person. These relatives have often progressed beyond the growth opportunities that Earth can provide. They are ready and free to move on to higher planes of spiritual evolution, but a few choose to remain on Earth in their spiritual form for a time, mentoring another soul to whom they feel a strong connection. See that young dark-haired woman exiting the cafe? At her shoulder is the soul of her great uncle. After her uncle had completed his current lifetime on Earth, which ended a few years before the woman's birth, his guides and he agreed that serving as her guardian would be ideal. He was perfectly suited to assist her in tackling her specific lessons and to be challenged himself in the process."[56]

The spiritual being at the young woman's shoulder was more clearly defined than the angels. Aislinn could make out the outline of the great uncle's clothing as well as his hairstyle. His light brown "hair" was parted to one side. As the woman walked towards the shoulder of the road to her car, the spirit turned towards Aislinn, and acknowledged her presence with a wink. Aislinn realized now what Pop meant when he explained that heaven was all there was. Right now, though on the physical Earth, she was still on the spiritual plane, in "heaven". Free from the limitations of her physical form, the truth was apparent: no separation between Earth and the spiritual plane existed.

What struck Aislinn most as she observed the spiritual guides was the calm, peaceful devotion they showed towards their charges. Aislinn only knew such compassionate care to be associated with the unconditional love a parent has for their newborn child. However, even the dedication shown by the best Earthly parent would be dwarfed by what she witnessed from these angels and guides. These beings knew the true worth of those they were guiding.

"If only people knew how they were being cared for and protected, so much pain would be eliminated." Aislinn reflected on how comforted she would have been after any of her recent losses had she acutely felt her guides' presence. Yet, as Pop had explained to her, that feeling of separation seemed somehow important for spiritual growth. Would she have grown as much through her grief had she not felt that she was alone in her struggle?

"No," Jesus responded. "Separation from your guides, from divine guidance, accelerates growth at a certain point in a soul's development. Part of the learning experience on your planet is working through the illusion of separation from God and valuing yourself and others in spite of it. Professional sports players' abilities are put to the test and perfected when they are playing on the road, jeered by the fans of the opposing team. They must develop deep confidence in both their skills and the strength of their team to succeed in such a situation. Though skills can still be developed when playing in front of cheering fans, the opposition experienced away from their hometown strengthens their confidence and sharpens their abilities. Just as carbon, given time and pressure, transforms into a beautiful diamond, your soul matures from the contrast and resistance experienced on Earth. However, just as the coach's voice can still be heard in the opponent's stadium, though more dimly because of the noise of the crowd, the presence and advice of your guides can still be felt while in your physical body if you quiet your heart and mind to listen."

Jesus' last point interested Aislinn. It seemed that some were more in tune with their spiritual "coaches" than others.

"Some people seem to be able to hear the voices of their guides clearly, or at least claim to. Is this true?" Aislinn inquired.

"Your Earthly bodies and minds are designed to provide a barrier to fully experiencing the spiritual plane, and this is the case for all humans on Earth," Jesus answered. "Your guides also provide a bit of that barrier, as they are limited to revealing only the guidance that is helpful for you to receive. However, you are correct; a person's awareness is ultimately up to the maturity of their soul and how much they choose to train their minds and bodies to be conscious of the spiritual. It is your soul's responsibility to open yourself to their presence, on the timeline that is right for you. Even within an Earthly body, near-full awareness is possible, if a soul's spiritual energy is high enough."

Jesus was always thinking three steps ahead of Aislinn and shifted their location to an experience that would illustrate his point. They were still on Earth, but this time in a large suburban office. Cubicles dotted with small potted plants and framed pictures lined the walls. A dark-skinned man in his thirties sat at a gray desk in a cubicle about halfway down one row, resting his forehead on his forefingers, attempting to hide the emotion displayed in his dark brown eyes. Not just one, but four angels surrounded this man; the other three angels were guardians of nearby souls who were not in need of immediate care.[57]

"What happened to him?" Aislinn asked.

"About ten minutes ago, Chris received a call from his father. His mother has brain cancer, late stage—only six weeks to live, per the diagnosis." A look of sadness was etched on Jesus' face. "It is her time and losing her will help him with a lesson he is here to learn. Still, it is never easy to see someone suffer. The angels have drawn near to him, for they know the pain this loss will cause. Chris and his mother have been inseparable for his entire life. She taught him both French and piano and shared her deep faith with him. Up until she began to experience the severe headaches induced by her illness, they would attend church together every Sunday, then enjoy a spirited debate in French over brunch. This loss will be hard on him. He will feel abandoned, especially that first Sunday after her passing. However, because of the strength of his spirit, he will feel the angels' presence, though he may not fully understand what he is experiencing. With the care that his family and friends will provide and the warmth of the love of the angels surrounding him, in time, he will grow stronger. His faith will deepen, and he will dedicate himself to sharing the love his mother showed him with others. For now, though, the feeling of loss is strong."

Jesus paused, his empathy for the suffering man washing over Aislinn. Her heart also went out to Chris. She knew much of the pain and grief he was experiencing firsthand. In her own times of loss, Aislinn remembered moments when she would feel strangely comforted. She, too, had not been abandoned, though she had been unaware of the presence of her guides.

"There's something else here I want you to see." Jesus nodded toward another man, just out of sight of Chris in the small hall between the cubicles. This man was younger—perhaps in his mid-twenties. He looked nervously at his grieving coworker, running his hand through his silky black hair, unsure of what to do. As he hesitated, a slightly older man, a tall, thin gentleman, accidentally bumped into the younger coworker. The tall man had been distracted by Chris' quiet sobs, but after a quick "excuse me," turned aside and walked briskly, his eyes focused a few cubicles ahead.

"What is worse," Jesus asked Aislinn, "A man who desires to help but in his inexperience fears failure, or one who knows just enough to realize he doesn't want to play the game?"

Aislinn could see the hesitant man's angel edge closer and knew the answer. Maybe this was the man's first time helping a stricken soul, but it certainly would not be his last. There was an unspoken quality to the man, something deep within him that spoke to a spiritual depth and maturity that the other had not had.

"His soul is strong," Jesus said, "He desires to reach out to Chris, but needs to gather the courage to overcome his fear of rejection."

The young man took a few tentative steps forward, then paused, brow slightly furrowed. His angel leaned forward so that he was touching the man's shoulder. Even from their place, several meters away, Aislinn could feel the waves of encouragement the angel was sending to the conflicted man.

"It's okay, John," she heard the angel whisper. "Chris needs you right now. You're not too young or unimportant. Just be there and listen. Be brave."

Aislinn watched as John looked slightly upwards, shook his head, shrugged, and moved towards Chris. He leaned over and rested a hand on Chris' shoulder. Chris started, surprised at the interruption of his deep thoughts.

John cleared his throat. "Hey man....want to go grab some coffee?"

Chris looked up and forced a smile. "Yeah...that would be awesome...thanks."

The angels hovering around Chris beamed, sharing a look of joy with John's guardian.

"What did he hea...," Aislinn started to ask.

"Nothing with his ears," replied Jesus. "Yet, he received the nourishment that only the angels could provide."

Jesus turned to face her, smiling. "To him, it sounded like his conscience, perhaps with a bit more force behind it. He could have easily ignored it—many times people do. For every moment like the one you just witnessed, there is another when the advice is ignored, to the detriment of both parties."

Aislinn thought of the cartoon of the little angel and devil perched on a person's shoulders. Jesus' lip twitched in amusement.

"You're wondering about evil? You might have noticed that there wasn't a horned demon hovering over John's other shoulder." Jesus laughed. Then, slowly his expression grew more serious. "However, there is reason for concern. Although angels far outnumber them, those beings whom you call evil do exist, and their influence is very real."

8

Hell

Their vantage point shifted. They were still on Earth, but this time in a bleak, poorly decorated hospital room. Aislinn was aware of the windows behind them, letting in beams of sunlight which provided the only bit of cheer to the room. A motionless body lay on the bed next to them. The body was male, in his mid-60's, with thinning salt and pepper hair that was greasy from several days spent in the hospital bed. A spirit dressed in a pristine business suit, but whose face was identical to that of the lifeless body, hovered nearby, visibly confused.

Jesus wrapped his arms around Aislinn. Though she couldn't feel his embrace like she could a human's, the feeling of love that surrounded and coursed through her was an amplified version of the emotions exchanged in an earthly hug.

"Steel yourself, Aislinn. Where we are going is a place you have never seen, nor should you ever want to. Yet, this experience will deepen your understanding of what love's absence, true despair, can lead to. I will not let go of you."

For the first time since her passing from her Earthly body, she felt a touch of fear. She continued to feel the comfort from Jesus' embrace but knew that he was holding back just a little, allowing part of her soul to be exposed. Aislinn looked at the man's spirit form, which still hovered beside the bed, looking increasingly befuddled and showing signs of frustration. He paced back and forth by the bedside, repeatedly reaching towards the breast pocket of his custom-fit dress shirt for a cell phone that was not there. The device, his principle means of communicating with others, was gone, and he was left alone, in threads that cost more than most cars.[58]

"Can he see us?" Aislinn asked.

"He should be able to, now that he is free of his body," Jesus explained, "but he is spiritually blind—his energy is too low to perceive us. All his life, he increasingly separated himself from the

Spirit and from love, the essence of us all. Daily he chose to ignore the guidance within him, the urgings to gratitude, service, and compassion, the urgings that would have allowed him to once again vibrate in harmony with God. He made decisions that prioritized what he perceived was his own well-being and made a place and a name for himself at the expense of others. To him, his clients were nothing more than placeholders in a calendar and a paycheck in the bank. His family and friends were burdens at best and objects to be used to add to his accomplishments at worse. His decisions led him away from his chosen path of learning that he had planned for himself as well as the truth of who he is. Yet, he did not start this way. Every Christmas until he was 12, he was the first one up to celebrate the wonder and magic of the day, just like every other boy on his block."

The man, still unable to locate his phone, looked down at the strange form in the bed. He couldn't figure out who the form was, nor did he care. His greater concern was getting out of this place. Clearly, he was well; there was no need to stay in this hospital a moment longer. He turned towards the hall, yelling for someone to help him.

Immediately, a response came. "Bob! We're out here. You need to hurry." Voices reverberated through the hall. They sounded friendly enough, but a hint of anxiety passed over Aislinn as she heard them. The voices did not have the depth or tone that Jesus' voice had, or Pop's for that matter; there was a hint of something demanding, uncaring.

The man took a few hesitant steps toward the voices.

"We don't have much time, Bob, please hurry." This time the voice took on a raspy quality, and it seemed that the being who uttered the words was quickly becoming impatient.

Bob's spirit moved more quickly toward the door of the hospital room and turned right, following the voices. As Jesus and Aislinn followed him, Aislinn noticed that the hall had begun to darken and fill with a fog-like substance. Bob looked behind him, uncertain as to what was happening. He could still make out the hospital room far behind him, but he was becoming acutely aware that this hall was no longer a part of the hospital.

"Where are we going?" he asked, worry causing his voice to waver.

"You'll see—come on—we don't have much time." The voices sounded increasingly impatient and even a bit angry. The light continued to fade, and Bob was forced to look down at his feet as he walked.

After what seemed like a very long time, Bob stopped. There was just enough light remaining to make out the figures of the beings whom the voices belonged to—they were starting to move out of the darkness into the dim, gray light. The beings had wings and strangely shaped horns. As they drew closer, Bob became more and more distraught. He realized that one of these beings was making fun of him, pointing to his wrinkled pants.

"Some form of armor that is. Surely he is invulnerable!"

Another horned being tried to quiet the mocker. "Shut up fool! No one cares to hear your stupid narration."

Bob kept turning around to look behind him, hopeful that he might see some landmark that he recognized. His panic increased.

"I want to go back—where am I? Who...who are you?"

The beings drew closer, their rough, reptilian-like skin as well as their malicious expressions now visible. "You're dead," one said, a smirk marking his face. "This is where you live now; you belong here with us."

One of the largest beings drew closer, its eyes glowing, an evil hunger dancing from one eye to the other.

"Abandon all of your hope, imbecile. No one is here for you, and the road back is even more horrifying than the road ahead of you. Accept your fate, cretin, and be forever tormented knowing that the only quarter offered will be equal to that which you have given over the course of your meaningless life."

It continued. "You deserve this, you filthy wretch," it said, digging its sharp teeth into the man's skin. The other beings, emboldened by the actions of their leader, also descended on Bob, shouting insults and tearing at his flesh with teeth and claws. They were like a mob, driven by unbridled brutality. Bob's cries of agony pierced Aislinn's heart as the evil beings physically devoured him.

Aislinn screamed and Jesus' embrace intensified.

"How can they do this? He doesn't even have a physical body!" she cried.

"Yes. Though he cannot truly be harmed, he believes it is possible. The beings are feeding on his fears and self-hatred. His belief that physical pain is possible and even deserved creates the illusion of physical destruction and the pain that goes with it."

For the first time since her death, Aislinn felt truly afraid, and the waves of peace and comfort that Jesus was sending through her were not enough to calm her. This was no review of past experiences, no movie. This was really happening to a fellow human, and one of the most powerful beings in the universe was simply watching. Aislinn knew Jesus was capable of stopping this and yet he just looked on, holding her, a bystander to this horror. Her fear quickly turned to anger. The part of her soul that Jesus had left open was searing with pain, as though a white-hot iron was being slowly laid across it.

The demons plucked the final sinews from Bob's legs, leaving the rest of his form for a future meal. They playfully picked the gristle from between their teeth and flicked it at one another, allowing the inedible 'meat' to fall unceremoniously onto the floor.

"How can you stand here and let this happen to him?!" Aislinn yelled, fighting against Jesus' emotional embrace to turn and face him. "No one deserves to go through this—I don't know what this man did during his life, but no offense warrants being treated like this!" She was furious, terrified, and panicked, despite Jesus' attempts to calm her. He allowed Aislinn to scream and her emotions to pour out unfettered, all the while keeping his emotional embrace firm and steady around her. Eventually she calmed enough to look up into his eyes. When she looked at his tear-streaked face, she knew Jesus understood—the pain in his eyes far exceeded that in her own.

Once she was emotionally steadied enough to hear him, Jesus spoke. "It is true. Nothing Bob could ever do would warrant this type of punishment. However, Bob believes that he deserves this treatment. He does not recognize who he is, and, even worse, does not believe in a God who could love him. Aislinn, I would give anything for this man, to prevent this suffering." Jesus showed her his palms, the nail holes now visible. "I already have." Aislinn quieted, slowly understanding.

"I gave my life for Bob, but I cannot force him to accept my gift," Jesus said. "We can lead the way, but we can never make a soul turn towards home and recognize who they are."[59]

Aislinn's heart filled with compassion for Bob, who was unable to reach out to the God who gave his life for him. "How do souls become this way?"

Jesus' eyes were filled with sorrow. "Bob and others here led lives that took them far from their true selves. Some vehemently denied that God exists. Others made choices that took them further into self-obsession and away from the guidance of the Spirit, continually rejecting the advice of their guides and separating themselves from all who cared for them. The most heart-breaking believe themselves to be unworthy of God's love.[60] In all cases, these souls are rejecting all help and we cannot force ourselves on them. This does not mean we have abandoned them." Jesus held her gaze for a moment longer, giving her time for her emotions to settle and her soul to anchor itself again to his peace.

"This is not the end of the story, Aislinn."

They shifted their point of view again. Now they were above Bob and what Aislinn assumed must be demons. As they looked down on him from a place of light above, Bob's screams of agony intensified, the demons moving on to the next course. Aislinn's heart, like Bob's spiritual body, was torn to shreds.

Jesus gently directed Aislinn's focus to the place where they were now located. She was shocked into silence by the sight—dozens of angels were suspended over the abyss, their light forms in stark contrast to the darkness of the pit beneath them. Tears were falling from their eyes as they watched and waited for Bob and others there with him, even those committing the torture, to look up to them.[61]

"What happens when someone does reach out to the angels?"

Jesus, feeling the pain that Aislinn felt for those suffering, was touched by the depth of her compassion.

"If they look up, believing that we are real, then they can see us and receive our love," Jesus explained. "We can come to their aid as soon as their hearts open, even a bit, to the divine. Yet the angels do not just wait for an opening. We do all that we can to reach them—everything that we can that would not deny them their freedom."

Jesus' words were hard to comprehend. "Wait," Aislinn said. "They are choosing this? That can't be."

"By rejecting love and holding on to fear and self-absorption, they *are* choosing this. A choice deferred is still a choice. Until their souls open to our help, any efforts on our part are futile."

He paused, choosing the best example to help Aislinn understand. "Just a few moments ago, you were very upset. What would have happened if I had tried to turn you to me while you were feeling that way?"

"I would probably just have become more angry."

Jesus nodded. "Even though, deep down, all you wanted was the knowledge that everything was okay, the assurance of the truth of my heart."

Aislinn nodded. All she had desired was Jesus' love at that moment, both for her and for Bob.

"So, what did I do?" Jesus asked.

"You were there with me, surrounding me with compassion until I calmed, until I was open to listening to you."

"Yes. I think you understand better now why the angels are here and what they are doing." Jesus motioned towards the right and their forms moved there. "Watch this soul—see how the demons are backing away, screaming? She has become open enough to God's love that the angels have reached her. They have been reminding her through her conscience of her love for God as a child.

"But the demon told Bob that the way back to the light was harder than the road further into hell," Aislinn said.

"This," Jesus noted, "is a half-truth, and a trick of the damned. Though the choice to surrender to God may be challenging at first, the journey back to God is far easier than its alternative. As you well know, as you grow to be more like your Father, you are always supported and guided by us. The demons frequently twist the truth. Their true food is not the flesh you see them consuming but rather convincing others to release any sense of hope and embrace the 'truth' that God has abandoned them."

Aislinn watched as the woman, her clothes and skin ripped apart, whispered God's name under her breath. The demons were slowly backing away—moving further from her with every utterance. This gave the woman courage. She began shouting the name of God, and slowly beginning to smile. Then she paused, realizing what was happening. A look of sudden inspiration and conviction came over her face.

Jesus stopped suddenly; a grin crept across his face. Then, after a second or two he said: "πρὸ πάντων δὲ τὴν εἰς ἑαυτοὺς ἀγάπην ἐκτενῆ ἔχοντες, ὅτι ἡ ἀγάπη καλύψει πλῆθος ἁμαρτιῶν." Aislinn, hearing the words in Greek, still understood the meaning—a verse from Peter's first letter, "Above all, love one another deeply, for love covers a multitude of sins."

Jesus' whole being shone forth with the delight he felt. "She just cried out for God to save her." Aislinn thought of the line in the Bible about heaven rejoicing more over one repentant sinner than ninety-nine righteous and watched as that joy played out in her Savior's eyes.[62]

Aislinn was by his side, feeling his deep compassion for the woman. The ugly beings who had been closing in on her were now almost out of sight, their horrid faces visibly pained.

"Why are the demons backing away?"

"They do not want God to see what they have become. They are unwilling to surrender to God and trust in God's forgiveness. When a soul reaches out to God, the demons first try to convince the tortured soul that the loving God the soul is beginning to hope in isn't real, but once they fail, they flee."

"God, save me!" the woman cried again at the top of her lungs.

The demons vanished entirely into the darkness at this, and an angel descended to her, carefully lifting her previously mangled body, which instantly was restored to wholeness. They rose to where the rest of the angels waited to embrace and welcome the woman home. Aislinn smiled broadly, the scene warming her soul. Then she thought about Bob.

"Does everyone eventually remember and return home?"

Jesus paused. "Many do. But there are a few who pull further and further from the truth, receding into the darkness that is the absence of God's love. Those beings are what you call demons." He smiled a sad, half-smile. "Yet even those are loved by God and may return, if ever they choose."[63]

9

The Mountain and the Core

They had returned to the forest. Aislinn needed time to simply be and enjoy the beauty and quiet of the woods after what they had just experienced. As she rested, she considered what she had grown up learning about those who did not believe in Jesus. She feared for them—would they also end up in that horrid place until they turned to the truth?

"You have many more questions." Jesus gave voice to her thoughts. "You wonder about the path of others—others who do not know me?" He welcomed her questions and rejoiced in her desire to learn.

"There is only one truth," Jesus explained. "All beings must journey to know and accept what is true. I am the truth and I embodied truth in my life on Earth. I bring that truth—the essence of the divine—to every planet I visit."[64]

Amazement gave way to horror behind Aislinn's eyes. "How many times have you..."

Jesus cut her off, saving her from having to voice such a dreadful question. "Don't worry, Aislinn. On many planets, I am welcomed and embraced. But your world needed my sacrifice to be free from the many burdens they laid on their own shoulders. Because of your planet's purposeful separation from the divine, the separation that allows you to grow so quickly, those on Earth struggle with guilt and fear. Many try to cope by trying to earn the love of God through needless sacrifices and a life tied to excessive laws and regulations. Others futilely compete for a better standing in God's sight. A standing, that, as you now know, does not exist. Not only did I show the way to right living through my example, but I offered myself as a final, perfect sacrifice, so that if any doubted their value in the Creator's eyes, he need only look to the cross. My death paved the way for humans to be able to forgive themselves, as well as each other."[65]

For Aislinn, the assurance of God's love through the cross helped her to lessen the number of hateful thoughts she had about herself. She remembered as a teen thinking that if Jesus loved her enough to give his life for her, then she must have worth. Jesus' sacrifice also gave her a reason to forgive others, as even her Earthly mind could understand that Jesus died for all, not just for herself. Yet Jesus had still not answered her question.

"What about those who do not know you or believe in you?"

"I taught truth while I walked the Earth," Jesus answered, "and I died to be a beacon of hope and truth to many. There is only one truth, the love of God. At the end of a lifetime on Earth, it is the willingness of the soul to turn towards God, the truth of who they are and all that is, that matters. However, whether a soul reaches that place through belief in my sacrifice or by an open heart to God and the Spirit through another path does not alter the end result. Any soul whose heart is open to truth will find it when they leave their physical form."[66]

They were now in front of a vast landscape dominated by a tall mountain. As in many situations in this realm, Aislinn could simultaneously take in different views of this natural wonder. She observed that there were several pathways snaking their way up the mountain, each with its unique landmarks and challenging obstacles. One path was composed of switchbacks, breaking the ascent into more manageable, gradual climbs, albeit making the trip much longer. Small trees lined this path, which was scattered with stones of a manageable size. They could be overcome with little effort. Another path was much steeper and direct, with large boulders blocking any obvious path. Climbers required ropes and other gear to make the ascent. Yet another face was snow-covered, with large drifts deep enough to bury a person, slowing the climbers. All paths led to the peak, which was obscured by the low-lying clouds that surrounded it.

"There are many pathways to truth," Jesus explained. "Each faith pathway has the essence of the divine within it and therefore all paths lead to me, though the traveler may not be aware of it." Aislinn understood the metaphor of the mountain as Jesus continued to explain. Each path harbored climbers from a different faith—Jews,

Muslims, Christians, Sikh, Hindi, and members of a dozen other religions that she was not as familiar with.

"If the climbers met to discuss their paths to the summit, they would hardly believe they were scaling the same mountain," Jesus explained. "Their journeys would be so disparate that they could easily convince themselves that they were climbing different mountains. And yet, they would eventually reach the same summit."

Jesus went on, "Followers of different faith paths have routes to God that seem irreconcilable. Even their views and descriptions of truth are vastly different. And yet, though no path is perfect, each captures a part of the ultimate reality. Remember how you learned that your soul, with the help and advice of others, selects the lessons and life path for that soul's time on Earth?"

Aislinn nodded, remembering one of the first lessons Jesus had taught her.

"As you planned the overview of your life, you and your guides chose a family and culture with the faith that would best assist you in meeting your life goals. Your previous lifetimes, individual soul traits, challenges, and strengths affected this placement. Each faith tradition has inherent disciplines and traditions that yield different benefits to souls. Just as the places of study and creative expression in the heavenly cities are designed to satisfy and celebrate different souls' unique qualities, so too are the faith traditions. Each tradition is tailored to the hearts of those who pursue it. The ideal faith background for a soul may change from one life to the next, or even from one phase of a single lifetime to another, based on that soul's unique characteristics, history, and goals for that lifetime."[67]

"So, there is no one faith that is best?" Aislinn asked.

"For any one soul, yes. But only because one path might be more suited to who they are and the lessons they are focused on than another. For instance, Christianity has a strong focus on the heart while the Hindu and Buddhist faiths emphasize disciplining the mind. All religions have value. All start with a direct revelation from God. However, over time, religions, led by humans with impure motives, distort this truth. Thus, each is correct about many aspects but also each misses the truth in some areas. Beings on your planet would draw much closer to the truth by sharing and building on each other's beliefs and experiences rather than attacking and breaking down the traditions of others."

Aislinn considered how the different faiths of her high school friends, one a Muslim, another a Sikh, led to rich conversations about their traditions and beliefs. However, both of those faiths seemed to be irreconcilable with her own. "But how can faiths so disparate, such as the Hindu and Christian faiths, be pursuing the same truth?"

"Each faith, in its own way, teaches its followers to turn from isolation and selfish desire and towards connectedness with and service to others and the divine. There are aberrations of these faiths that have shifted far from their origins. In these there is inevitably a push towards self-centeredness and disregard for others. However, the root of all faiths is pure and leads to truth. Perhaps seeing firsthand the truth all these paths pursue may assist in your understanding."

Jesus grew silent, almost as he was before their journey with Bob. She felt as though Jesus and the lessons of the spiritual plane were about to challenge her again.

"Just as your journey with Bob showed you how far your soul has come, where we are going next will stretch your understanding of the glory of the adventure ahead of you. It is time to experience the totality of who I am and what you will one day become."

Aislinn felt a complex mix of apprehension and excitement for what Jesus had alluded to. Throughout her experience on the spiritual plane, with the exception of her time in the hellish realm, beautiful, white light suffused all that she saw. The light had no physical source from which it radiated and there were no shadows cast. Instead, light energy seemed to be the very fabric of all that existed here. Certainly, those entities who were more spiritually evolved appeared brighter, but all beings and even all matter shone. This was far more beautiful and wonderful than she had imagined that heaven would be. It was simply inconceivable that anything could be more pure, perfect, or complete. Yet she trusted Jesus' words and her anticipation grew.

They slowly rose from the ground on which they stood. As they rose, the light became brighter and more intense. She saw orbs traversing the plane before her, some moving purposefully towards the light, some away.[68]

"What are the orbs?" Aislinn questioned. "Are they more highly evolved souls, like those I saw in the city?"

"Yes. They are beings like you and me. Some are leaving to fulfill various purposes; others are returning to their source."

As they neared the orbs, Aislinn heard music—the orbs were singing. The music was unlike any Earthly song. At first it sounded like a comforting, soft hum, but as they drew closer, she began to understand the origin of the stories of heavenly choirs. Their song was a loud, glorious chant--a sound that she could both hear and feel, filling Aislinn to her core with joy. For a moment, Jesus kept them slightly removed from the song, and she understood how, on Earth, the drawing of a bow across a string could cause a heart to ache or how the blast of a horn in a national anthem could usher men and boys off to war. All of these Earthly vibrations paled in comparison to the call this song had on her soul. As she heard and felt the music of these beings and experienced their beauty, she joined with them, overcome.

"Much in the same way that you cannot tell your heart to stop beating, or that you cannot command your soul not to love, these entities simply cannot override the urge to join in the song of gratitude to and praise of their creator." Jesus explained."[69]

Jesus and Aislinn continued to rise, the song growing louder, vibrating within them, until they were within the light itself. Here, Aislinn still existed, but, at the same time, she had blended seamlessly with the light. She no longer desired to control what would happen. Desire itself was impossible here, yet she did not cease to be an independent entity. Her form was disappearing, as was Jesus'. They were simply one with the light. Borders faded, like grains of sugar dissolving into water. Where once there were multiple individual parts, now they were one, giving of their unique natures to the complete glory of the whole. That whole, the light, was perfection and goodness beyond anything that could be conceived of on Earth.[70]

Still they rose, maintaining the forms they had assumed when melding with the light. Now they were not just love, but also complete and perfect intelligence. Aislinn had an awareness of such immense amounts of knowledge—she came to see the great challenges of philosophy, science, and mathematics, not as divine riddles, but as human constructs, feeble attempts to explain the perfection of God, puzzles and conundrums whose answers showed the mastery of the creator. Math had been easy enough for her during her school days, but now she had a deep appreciation for its pure, sublime beauty—she saw and understood the framework of creation.[71] Its simple elegance was overwhelming. Oh, and the joy—she understood why the light beings sang—Aislinn felt as if she could not contain the glory of what was within and enveloping her.

And still they rose higher. Here the vibration was so high, the souls here so pure, that the energy was far more than she could bear. Instead of feeling the sense of comfort and peace she had known elsewhere in heaven, she felt something akin to pain from the high vibration, to which her own soul was not in tune. Pop had explained that her soul would need to evolve to be at home in the higher levels of heaven. Aislinn understood clearly that she was far from ready for the energy held in this space. Here was the location of creation—new souls and new energies were born. Just as souls close to the core burst forth in song, souls here created from the intensity of the energy within them. Unbound on the spiritual plane by time, Aislinn witnessed spectacular galaxies spinning into being, their colors beautiful to behold. As beautiful as witnessing creation itself was, she could not bear the disparity between the energy here and her own. Jesus, aware of her soul's struggle, quickly removed them and they slowly descended, returning this time to the peace of the wooded garden.

Aislinn sat on the bench, overwhelmed by what she had felt. The power and immensity of the highest level of heaven—the very essence of God—was beyond words. Aislinn was silent and still, grateful to once again be where she was comfortable. Jesus sat by her side, without any need to rush her.

After a considerable period of resting with all that she had experienced, a question occurred to Aislinn. The very fabric of the universe, as she had just witnessed, was pure, unconditional love, and yet she knew that evil still existed, evil at a level that surpassed even what she had experienced in her body. Pop and Jesus had both explained the importance on Earth of the illusion of separation from God for the soul's growth. Yet she wondered why that illusion had to result in the hell where Bob had found himself. She wondered how a perfect author of life could allow anything but good to exist.

"How can evil exist among all this beauty and goodness?" she asked.

"Dear Aislinn, evil exists precisely because there is good."[72]

"I don't understand."

"A truly loving creator would never control his creation. And good cannot exist in all its fullness or be appreciated for what it is without the contrast of its opposite."

Aislinn considered this. It did make sense that free will required there being two or more options from which to choose. She could accept the existence of evil for that reason alone—but there was still the question of Earth. There, even on the most perfect, idyllic day, conflict and evidence of the marring of that short-lived perfection was consistently apparent. Trash strewn next to the path in a beautiful park, voices raised in anger, families and nations divided, disease, natural disasters—all gave witness to a world fraught with evil. The ratio of evil to good seemed much, much higher on Earth than heaven, and even much higher than any planet she had visited.

"How can so much evil exist on my planet? It seems Earth is filled with temptation and evil, yet here good is almost all there is," Aislinn noted.

Jesus nodded. "God allows evil to exist, as he would not be truly good if he did not. However, God does control where evil can take hold. You are correct, in almost all that exists, what is good vastly exceeds what is evil."[73]

A large bowl appeared before them, filled with brilliant, translucent marbles. The immense bowl contained upwards of a thousand of these spheres. Yet there was one black marble mixed in with the others, just barely visible at the bottom right side of the bowl.

"Love is almost all there is," Jesus stated, gesturing towards the bowl, and yet..."

The bowl now contained a very different ratio—for every three shimmering, clear marbles, one black was mixed in.

"This is the amount of contrast to the true nature of God allowed on your planet," Jesus said.

Aislinn stared, horrified. "But, why? What did we do to deserve to live in such a world?"

Jesus looked down on her kindly, with sympathy in his eyes. "Remember that you chose to live your life there."

She shook her head in disbelief. She still struggled to believe that she had freely chosen the details and trials of her life. Jesus was silent, patiently watching and waiting for Aislinn to consider and integrate all that she had learned. After much thought, she carefully responded.

"I know we are on Earth to learn. Could it be beneficial to be faced with the daily contrast and temptation in order to grow towards love and goodness?"

Jesus' form radiated his approval. "That is very perceptive, Aislinn. Often souls choose to live many lifetimes on planets such as Earth earlier on in their development. Since each soul must forget their previous lives and the truth of who they are when born on Earth, they are open to the influence of both the essence of the divine and its contrast. Combined with the illusion of separation from God, this spurs souls to faster discovery and development of love and wisdom.[74] Through trial and error and the experiences of many lifetimes, they discover the consequences of their choices. Most souls begin to increasingly make choices that prioritize service and compassion. They wake up to the truth of their interconnectedness with all beings and find their fulfillment in giving of themselves to others. However, a small number of souls also gradually wake to the truth of who they are but instead use this truth to manipulate others for their own self-benefit. These souls, after many lifetimes serving as the contrast to the truth, eventually come back home. Regardless of their final choice, all develop into fully unique beings who have a deep appreciation for who they are and their place in creation. It is the contrast present on Earth combined with the illusion of separation from God that gives souls the challenges and difficult choices needed to learn to become more like the creator."

The scene shifted again. Jesus and Aislinn were now watching as a small boy climbed up a steep, rocky hillside. The young boy, with his father beside him, worked his way to the top. His father was slowly and purposely noting each foot and hand placement, even helping to place the boy's feet as they climbed. He supported his son's weight, propelling the toddler's body onwards and upwards.

"The boy is making great progress and probably enjoying himself," Jesus commented, "but he will be slow to learn to climb independently, unless…"

Aislinn looked to her left—the father was now crouched behind a large tree, watching his son from a distance, hidden from the boy's view. She could see the frustration in the boy's eyes as he slid backwards multiple times, struggling to find his grips. The father didn't take his eyes off his son, ready to jump in if ever the struggle became too great. The boy believed himself to be alone. The father had judged rightly, and the boy's determination was strong; his son was up to the challenge. The child became increasingly sure of himself as he drew closer to the top.

"He knew that his son needed to do this on his own to truly learn the skill," Aislinn observed.

"And yet the father never left the boy alone. Neither do we leave you alone."

The boy came sliding down the back side of the hill, his path eased by a coating of leaves, then turned the corner to make the climb again, a large smile spread across his face.

"You grow and learn best in opposition. When you are seemingly alone in the midst of the challenge, it may not seem worth the sacrifice, but your reward in heaven is great."

_10_

Rescue

Dave walked out onto the beach, surfboard in hand. Aislinn had tried to be quiet that morning while dressing, but, despite her years as a dancer, graceful was not the word he would pick to describe the muttering and hopping about that had woken him. He had feigned sleep until she left, then slowly got ready himself, figuring twenty minutes or so would be enough lead time for her to enjoy the ocean.

As he made his way to the waves, immediately something struck him as off. There was a huddle of early morning beachgoers near the surf, their focus out in the distance. As Dave neared them, his eyes followed the general direction of their gaze. Two rescue swimmers were far out in the surf, their red rescue cans bobbing in the surf. Dave dropped his board, his heart plummeting. Aislinn was not in the huddle, which meant...

"Oh, God, no. Please, no," Dave cried, sprinting to the edge of the surf. The rescuers, one man and one woman, were supporting a woman's limp body in the waves as the rescue line pulled the swimmers to shore. As they neared, Dave sunk to his knees. The lifeless body belonged to his wife.

As soon as they had pulled Aislinn's body far enough up the beach, the female rescuer immediately began CPR while the man rummaged through their supplies, providing her with the necessary equipment. He turned briefly and saw Dave's clear distress.

"Are you by chance...?"

"Her husband." Dave's eyes didn't leave Aislinn's face. He was looking for any sign of life. "What happened?"

Without looking up, the swimmer explained. "Her surfing partners called in the emergency fifteen minutes ago. We'll do everything we can, man. Let's pray she's one of the lucky ones."

Dave didn't need to be told twice. If there was a God, he needed him now.

11

Connection

Jesus transported them back to the open field where Aislinn had found herself after her transition out of her body. The quiet sound of the rippling stream in the distance, the beautiful light energy, and the smell and flavor of the grass once again filled her senses. Aislinn knew that this was no coincidence. After all she had experienced, she was back at the location where she started, with a decision to make. Jesus was facing her, his gaze holding hers.

"You already know what you must do." His eyes were still focused on hers, his expression infused with sympathy. He knew both what her final decision would be and how difficult a decision it was for her to make.[75]

This heaven held the fulfillment of everything she had spent her Earthly time longing and searching for. It seemed inconceivable that any soul would choose to return, and yet, as Jesus advised, she knew that she must. She felt him withdraw ever so slightly, giving her space to feel how she handled a tiny gap between his energy and hers.

"You know that your work and learning on Earth is not yet complete and that other souls would struggle with their own journeys without you," Jesus said. "Yet leaving the spiritual plane is not easy. I hope you will take comfort in what I will show you next."

They were above the Earth, its beauty astonishing to behold as it slowly rotated, suspended in space. Streams of light sprang from points all over the globe. The blue sphere glowed, covered by these beams of light.

Aislinn looked on, absorbed in the beauty of the Earth's glow and curious as to what she was seeing. "What are these lights?" she asked.

"Each beam of light is a prayer, a reaching out of the soul beyond itself. Some are requests on behalf of a loved one or themselves for blessing or healing. Many are heart-filled expressions of praise and gratitude. Any one of these beams of light may seem insignificant on its own. Collectively, however, they have the power to transform the Earth."[76]

The beauty of the illuminated Earth touched Aislinn's heart. She could feel an energy field created by the prayers enveloping the planet, the prayers seeming to have a protective and perhaps transformative power.

Jesus drew Aislinn's attention closer in. Her focus shifted from the globe as a whole to the origin of one particular beam. She saw a man sitting on the cement stoop of his house, hands draped over his knees, his eyes searching the night sky. He was speaking the words aloud, just under his breath, a prayer for his daughter. Bright streams of light flowed from the father's heart as he prayed. Aislinn noticed the diaphanous strand that connected him to his little girl pulsing and growing brighter. Inside the house, the young girl, about eleven or twelve, was asleep on her bed, her curly black hair splayed out in all directions across the pillow as she dreamed. Aislinn thought that the daughter's energy, like her father's, seemed to brighten as the prayer's energy reached her.

"Yes," Jesus said, confirming her observation. "Prayer transforms both the soul of the one praying as well as those prayed for."

Jesus shifted her focus to another beam. Its source was a middle-aged woman. She was walking with a few others from her community along a dirt path, low-lying vegetation covering the ground on each side, an empty pot to collect water balanced gracefully on her head. As she walked, she hummed a song. Aislinn felt the woman's emotion as she gave voice to what she felt within, gratitude for the natural beauty that surrounded her and joy in sharing the daily journey with her companions.

"Though the direction of a prayer of gratitude is straight to the creator, the father and giver of all gifts, the power of such prayers raises the energy of all souls, especially those on Earth. This is true of other prayers as well. The stronger the prayers of any kind, provided they come from a heart connected to the Spirit, the more connected to the divine the Earth will be and the more beautiful life on Earth will become."[77]

Aislinn continued to gaze at the luminous, twinkling sphere. Her focus moved from one beam to another as she took in the immense positive power and transforming energy of the prayers. Suddenly, one particular streak of light came to the forefront. Aislinn followed the strand as it came from the Earth and realized that this prayer's destination was her own soul. As she studied the strand more closely, the light transformed into Dave's likeness. Aislinn was startled by his anguished appearance. Though the power of the prayer was positive, Dave was clearly in pain. His eyes were wide and panicked as he gaped at Aislinn's lifeless form below him.

"Please Aislinn, don't leave me," Dave cried. "I don't know what I'd do without you. God, please, I need a miracle." His hands covered his face, and his body shook with intense grief.

As Aislinn received her husband's prayer, she felt an uncanny sense of dedication and confidence, his prayer empowering her. Her decision had already been made—ever since she knew that it was her duty to return. But now, more than ever, she was emboldened by a sense of purpose, mixed with her ever-present compassion for others. She knew both intuitively and through Jesus' teachings that the journeys of those she cared for on the physical plane depended on her return. Dave, of course, had a journey intimately connected with hers. There were also her mother and father who should not have to bear the loss of a second daughter. Finally, her students' faces filled her consciousness. There were so many she could impact with the truth that was now firmly implanted within her. Though she still did not want to leave the spiritual plane, her choice was clear.

"I will go back..." she hesitated, unsure of her next words, "but I need help."

Jesus' head tilted slightly to one side, and he bent closer to Aislinn. "You know we never leave you, Aislinn."

"Yes, but, if I go back, will I remember this?"

"Some of it. There are elements you will forget because remembering those bits will hinder rather than help you on your Earthly journey."

At this, Aislinn remembered Jesus' injunction that she not know more about her future children, as such information would impede her growth. She could now see how painful future events—the passing on of her parents, husband, or children, future illnesses or world catastrophes—would be harmful to know about in advance. Just as a child dreads the pinprick of an immunization for days, the dark clouds in her mind would increase her suffering from a painful event many times over. Yet so much of what she experienced here should help, not hinder her growth.

Jesus heard her thoughts. "Even positive knowledge can be a barrier to growth, Aislinn. Positive future experiences are also designed for your growth, even though those lessons may be more enjoyable. Knowing about certain challenges and experiences beforehand would be like seeing the test and memorizing the questions ahead of time. However, even more importantly, remembering too much of the nature of the spiritual plane would interfere with the growth that comes through your separation from the divine on Earth."[78]

He continued. "Even what you do remember will make certain aspects of earthly life more challenging."

This last bit was something she was already well aware of. She remembered returning to college after a weekend retreat, faced with the juxtaposition of the peace and joy within her from the time away and the high-pressure, fast-paced campus environment she had just returned to. In addition to reconciling the peace within her with the stressful environment around her, she also struggled to communicate her transforming experiences and new outlook to those who did not share her faith. She imagined that her return to the physical plane would bring similar challenges, amplified many times over. Aislinn was choosing to return primarily out of a sense of duty and compassion for her family. She feared the sense of loss from leaving heaven. She openly wondered whether her grief would quickly decline or erode away slowly, over the period of months or years.

"Your transition will not be easy," Jesus said, confirming her concern. "It will take time. But you will retain knowledge that is rare on Earth. Knowing the truth of who you are and having a sense of your purpose will eventually allow you to thrive."[79]

Aislinn understood that all that she saw here had changed her to the core. Perhaps more importantly, it had changed her conception of what her core was. No longer would she fear death or be frozen by suffering and loss. She would know the general purpose of her life—to grow in love and wisdom—and would take comfort in knowing that her guides and the angels were ever-present and ready to come to her aid. However, she would struggle to explain all that she experienced and how she had changed to others. Aislinn also feared that she might too easily get pulled back into the concerns of the world. She did not want to return to her former ways, to fall back into fear and into her belief in separation from God.

"Will I be able to connect with the spiritual plane more easily now that I know the truth?" Aislinn asked.

"Yes," Jesus said. "The fabric of everything, both here and on Earth, is love.[80] All that you see around you is created from the energy of the divine. It is no different on Earth. You have already seen that you are surrounded on Earth by angels and guides, though your body cannot feel their presence. In the same way, everything on Earth, from the rocks to the plants and the animals are, at their core, made of the same essence as everything here on the spiritual plane. It is possible for you to learn to connect to this energy while on Earth, even while in your physical body. In doing so, you will feel an echo of heaven."

It did not surprise her when, once again, their surroundings shifted. Jesus rarely relied on words alone as he delivered his lessons. They were on Earth, high on a tree-covered ridge. Tall maple and birch trees graced the mountainside, almost entirely obscuring their view of the adjacent ridge. It was late afternoon, and the air was warm, a gentle breeze gracing their spiritual forms. In the distance, thunder echoed through the valley, a single beat elongating into a long roll as the sound passed from ridge to ridge, the ripple of the vibration moving gradually away from them, dimming to a brief silence. The wind began to build in strength, passing from treetop to treetop, the leaves seemingly handing the energy from branch to branch. As the sky turned to dark gray with a lingering hint of blue, the first of the raindrops began to fall, their tiny splashes marking the earth below them. Seconds later, the thirsty ground had soaked up all but a small remnant of the water, only a moist circle remaining on the soil's surface. Aislinn silently watched as the drops fell and were absorbed by the dirt. As the intensity of the rain increased, the drops overlapped, overwhelming the earth's ability to instantly receive them. Aislinn took in the majesty of the scene, though she was unclear as to the message Jesus desired to convey.

"Did you notice how the wind and the thunder seemed to pass through the valley and along the mountainside, handing the energy from tree to tree and ridge to ridge?" Jesus asked.

Aislinn smiled. "It was as if the trees and the mountains were singing, passing the notes through nature's choir."

Jesus nodded his agreement. "The song of the wind and the thunder is a beautiful outpouring of gratitude and joy to the creator. As it is expressed in creation, love is a glorious dance of giving and receiving. The energy is passed generously on from one form or entity to another. The air surrounding one tree branch gives the energy of the wind to the next, which receives it and passes it on once more. The same is true of the thunder, sound energy being received and freely given time and time again. Nothing is grasped, all is shared freely, from the sun's rays, to the wind, to the thunder."

"The rain too?"

"Of course. The rain is a gift to the thirsty ground, which takes what it needs and returns the remainder to the air to be given elsewhere, perhaps even as the morning dew the next day. When you look closely enough, the fingerprints of God are overwhelming."

As the rain continued to intensify, the drops came so rapidly that they fell in sheets. The wind escalated. It stampeded through the trees, bending them over with its strength. One older, weaker tree gave way, its large form tumbling to the earth with a crash, the roots ripping free from the ground and its trunk crushing the few young, budding saplings nearby.

Jesus saw Aislinn's puzzled expression and explained. "Even death is part of this beautiful dance. The trees, having throughout their lives taken from the Earth for their well-being, freely give of their physical being to nourish the lives of others. Death and transformation are a triumphant finale in the symphony of life, an act of surrender and giving to nourish the whole. New life is born in the wake of what has passed on."

"The Earth itself is intertwined beautifully with the divine, a masterpiece of love and wisdom," Jesus continued.[81] "Consider the intelligence inherent in the natural forest fires on the Earth. Every few years, a quick burn will naturally clear out the flammable underbrush, making way for new life and preventing larger fires from taking hold. Because of the necessary illusion of separation, much of this has been forgotten by humans. However, you, Aislinn, have been graced with a greater ability to remember and to begin to connect back to the divine on Earth."

The storm had ended and, as the sun dropped below the peaks of the distant mountains, the first stars appeared. Time sped quickly by before them, the points of light multiplying until the sky was ablaze with the canvas of the night sky.

"Look at the stars, Aislinn. During the day, the light from them still touches your eyes, but you are unaware of it; the sun's brightness overwhelming those faint points of light. The sun blinds you to the reality of the vastness of the universe. Just as the sun blocks the light of the stars, your mind is designed to block out much of the truth of the spiritual realm. But the heart of the divine surrounds you always, even though you cannot see the spiritual realm with your eyes."[82]

Aislinn took in the beauty of the night sky. Towards the center of the sky, the Milky Way's thick band of light was prominent. The stars at the center of the luminescent band were a bit fuzzy, blending one into another. She knew that if viewed through a telescope, the detail of each star could be seen. As she considered this, she thought back to her transition from Earth to heaven. When she left her physical body, her consciousness had expanded. Everything was clearer and more vivid, just as the stars were clearer when viewed through the telescope. Her ability to "see" and perceive reality was enhanced significantly.

In addition to her telescope-like ability to perceive detail regardless of distance, on the spiritual plane she was also able to take in all of her surroundings at once. Images blended with sound, taste, and smell, her senses merging into one integrated yet still highly detailed experience. On the physical plane that she would soon be returning to, not only were her senses less vivid, but only one or two senses at a time could be the focus, as if some information were being filtered out from the whole. Jesus had hinted that this was caused by the mind somehow.

"Is the mind a type of filter?" she asked.

Jesus was quick to respond. "In a way. On Earth the mind sorts and selects what to take in, including sensory information and the knowledge and experiences of the universe. Your mind is like an old AM/FM radio. A radio has two modes: one that detects amplitude modification and another that detects frequency modulation. Yet, like your senses, the two modes cannot be used at the same time, nor can multiple channels be heard clearly simultaneously. By controlling the amount and form of energy and information you can take in at any moment, the mind limits your connection to your spiritual origin. This is as God planned."[83]

Aislinn thought the comparison accurate. Sometimes on Earth, she did feel as though her mind were continually switching channels, if not bandwidths.

"The mind is a beautiful tool, Aislinn," Jesus continued. "Consider this comparison: On Earth, it is sometimes beneficial for a young person to leave their home and family for a short time in order to determine their true values and desires. The family still provides love and guidance to the youth, but the young person can more easily choose the experiences that reflect who they are without the direct influence of the voices and opinions of home. The youth, without the protection of the family, also learns quickly which choices lead to pain and struggle and which to the outcomes they desire. In the case of the transition to the physical plane, the mind creates the separation from heaven so that souls can choose their own pathways and learn the hard lessons of love and wisdom without the ever-present influence of heaven. Souls become more fully the unique expressions of the creator that they are, learning through trial and error, experimenting with various opportunities for self-expression, and facing the consequences of their actions, both positive and negative. It is only an illusion of separation, however. No one is ever truly alone or separate from God."[84]

Aislinn thought about her own Earthly experience. She had the opportunity to pursue dance and music, as well as her love for literature. She had felt leadings in these areas, a desire for the arts planted within her, but it was dimmer than the guidance she received on the spiritual plane. Thus, she was free to more fully engage in a wide range of experiences, from singing to dance to an unsuccessful foray into gymnastics. Because of the softened connection to her guides, she knew more fully what brought joy to her heart. She also had to learn the hard way the choices that brought happiness and pain to herself and others, a harder but more impactful learning than she could have received here on the spiritual plane.

"So, on Earth we can still access everything that is here, just more dimly?" Aislinn clarified.

"Yes. You already know that there are spiritual beings who are continually by your side, supporting you, even when you cannot see or sense them. Yet, with practice, if you will it, you can increase your ability to communicate with your guides and sense the spiritual energy that is the fabric of the physical plane."

Jesus paused and his expression became more intense. "However, I would give a word of caution. Just as you can become more in tune with the spiritual plane while on Earth, it is equally true that you can choose to ignore the guidance of heaven and block out the presence of the divine.[85] Souls such as Bob made such choices, much to their detriment. You must be vigilant regarding your will, Aislinn. You must continually choose to draw closer to the divine; the mind must be trained to receive the guidance of the Spirit."

Aislinn remembered Jesus telling his disciples something similar in the Garden of Gethsemane. Jesus knew of what was to come—his crucifixion—and chose vigilance in prayer over sleep. He urged his followers to do the same, aware that withstanding temptation takes practice and significant effort. Just desiring it, as Peter did that night, was not enough.

Jesus nodded, pleased that Aislinn was able to make the connection. "The spirit is willing, but the flesh is weak,"[86] he said.

12

Mind Training

Aislinn took Jesus' words of caution to heart. Witnessing the agony of Bob was enough to ensure that she stayed diligent in drawing close to God. However, what she felt most now was hope. There were ways she could grow to be more in touch with her guides and with the love she experienced in heaven as she matured on Earth.

"What can I do once I am back in my body to train my mind in this way?" she asked.

Jesus was quick to answer, expecting her question. "First, spend time in silence each day. Though there are times when learning independently is best, we are always reaching out to you, ready and willing to help you along your journey. As you spend time in silence, listening, your ability to hear our wisdom and feel the embrace of our love will strengthen."[87]

"By times of silence and listening, do you mean something like meditation?"

"Something akin to that, yes. The power of silent communion with God, a form of what many call meditation, was what I relied on while on Earth. Like you, I was in a physical body and had to work with a mind that filtered out much of the guidance and love of heaven. My time of silence with my heavenly Father allowed me to reconnect and have the power of the Father within me."

Aislinn remembered the limitations of her mind that held her back on Earth. Given what Jesus was able to do in his physical body, she struggled to believe that he had the same barriers as she did on Earth.

"But your miracles—how could any soul, no matter how great, work through the barrier of the mind in that way?" Aislinn asked.

"Didn't I say that you would be able to do just as I did, and even greater things?[88] I had all the limitations that you did in your body, Aislinn. However, I remembered who I was and willed strongly to reconnect to the kingdom of heaven. I spent hours each morning in quiet prayer with my Father.[89] That time was essential to allowing the Spirit of God to work through my limited form. It is a choice—you will be connected back to heaven to the degree that you will it to happen and make choices to bring that connection into being."

Aislinn was amazed by the power of Jesus' promise—that she could be almost as connected to God as Christ himself? However, something wilted within her at the thought of the dedication required—two hours of silent communion with God seemed more than she was ready for.

Jesus laughed, his face lighting up as he sensed the battle within her. "I tell you what is possible, Aislinn, not what is expected. Even a few minutes each day, preferably in the morning, will do wonders to bring some of the joy and love of heaven to your Earthly life."

Jesus' laughter settled into a calmer smile as he gave a word of caution. "Be aware not to become complacent though, content with the significant gains in awareness you will initially make. You may feel that connection to the spiritual plane more quickly; connection will take less time through practice. But be cautious: do not take the newly freed time for impotent endeavors or sunken investments into fruitless philosophical matters. Instead, use that time wisely to journey deeper into the heart of the Divine and to open yourself to the Spirit's work within you."

Unlike the previous word of caution, this warning would be one Aislinn would struggle with. On the physical plane she felt pulled in many directions. Any excuse to shorten the time spent doing something that her mind viewed as "unproductive" would cross her mind, often pulling her from her time of prayer. She would need to be disciplined and dedicated to connecting with the Spirit, valuing that time above all else.

"There is nothing more important, Aislinn," Jesus said, agreeing with her thoughts. "That is why I taught that spending time in connection to God was the one thing, the only thing, that truly matters.[90] Though communion with the divine is the practice of highest importance, there are others that will help you along your journey. It is beneficial to continually seek God's true wisdom by reading and engaging with those who have walked the path in the past. However, even this time well spent must be tempered with prayer and listening from your soul. You must be careful to ensure that what you learn aligns with your inner compass, the wisdom within you. The Bible is a beautiful place to begin study for many, especially given your Christian background; it is a handbook to your home and the truth you have experienced here."

Aislinn considered what she had been taught about the "Good Book." She knew of the many Christians who took every word literally—a literal six days of creation, Adam and Eve, the Flood, and the bit about the sun stopping in the sky.[91] Scientific-minded believers, on the other hand, struggled with this literal interpretation. In her Lutheran upbringing, many saw these stories primarily as spiritual parables.

"The Bible is filled with spiritual truth," Jesus continued, answering her question. "For this, it can be trusted. Read it as a map to your home and a handbook for your soul."[92]

"Some of what is within its pages must be more than just symbolic."

Jesus' mouth shifted, a smirk on his face. "Well, I'm real." His face then grew a bit more serious. "There are many portions that are literally true, but just as it is not worth spending the time and effort to discern the reasons for another's trials or how evolved another soul is, it is futile to concern yourself with what is an accurate recording of events and what should be seen as a parable. Instead, look to what speaks to your soul and allow this wisdom to both remind you of your identity and shape you into the more evolved soul you are becoming."

Aislinn nodded. She remembered battling as a teen with the teachings of Jesus in the New Testament. Many seemed far beyond what she could incorporate into her life and altogether the teachings simply overwhelmed her.

Hearing her thoughts, Jesus responded, "Each of my teachings requires years of practice to fully grasp and work into your life. Tackling them all at once is not as effective as working with them one at a time and watching your mindset, life, and world transform. Ultimately, all my teachings tie to the most important command I have given you here and in my time on Earth—love. With every teaching you embrace, you grow closer to becoming the embodiment of the divine on Earth—who you are meant to become."[93]

Aislinn remembered that Jesus taught that the commandment to love God, self, and neighbor completely summed up the law and the prophets. From that perspective, any individual teaching would lead back to love.

He continued. "Take the command to not worry about your life, to trust God to take care of you.[94] If you know your value in the eyes of God, you will trust him to provide what you need to complete your Earthly mission, freeing you to focus your energy on growing your soul while supporting others in their journeys. Likewise, my command to not harbor anger in your heart helps you to live in connection to other beings, to recognize those strands that tie our souls to all others."[95]

Aislinn realized the truth of this. When she released her anger, she did strengthen her bonds with others. When she put her trust in God to care for her, she was more able to invest in caring for others. Even one of Jesus' teachings, taken to heart, could dramatically improve her ability to connect compassionately to others.

When Jesus sensed Aislinn had grasped this truth, he continued. "But don't just look at my words; I was a living example of wisdom. Watch and learn from how I spent my days among you. I spent hours each day in prayer and solitude, seeking my Father's will. Like the Earth itself, I freely received and gave love throughout my life. I graciously received from my Earthly parents and my spiritual teachers, as well as from my Father in Heaven. Then, in turn, I gave of myself. I lived as a servant, even to my own mother and father. I lived a life of obedience to the plan set out for me and even laid down my life, so that others could have freedom and abundance on the physical plane. Finally, I lived a life of simplicity, in harmony with the Earth and as much as was possible, with man. I know how hard it is to live in the remembrance of who you are—I too have lived through the struggles on Earth, in large part to show you the way."

Aislinn considered how her priorities would look when she returned. By following Jesus' words and example, she imagined she would live a simpler, slower pace of life with a heightened focus on her connection with God and on human relationships.

"I am not the only one you can learn from," Jesus clarified. "There are other souls who have gone before you, many wearing the robes of different nations, as well as role models from other faith backgrounds who are wonderful teachers. Read their words. Listen to what they have to say. Most importantly, learn from their actions."[96]

Jesus paused, letting Aislinn take this in. "Lastly, to connect better to the divine energy that surrounds you, become more aware of your thoughts. Through your thoughts, you draw your soul closer to or further away from God. Remember the power of the prayers that you witnessed and how these prayers connect you to your spiritual brothers and sisters on Earth as well as to the love that is all around you. Thoughts of gratitude, focusing on the beauty in creation and in others, noticing the magnificence of your own being—the more you try to see the divine in all that surrounds you and express gratitude for it, the more you will be able to recognize the spirit of God in all things."

Jesus' words reminded Aislinn of the prayers of love and gratitude that caused the Earth to glow. She treasured that image of the Earth alive with the energy of the prayers. Aislinn also thought of the souls closer to God bursting into joyful songs, songs from hearts overflowing with gratitude, overcome by the glory of God that surrounded them. Just thinking about these experiences from the spiritual plane brought forth its own wave of gratitude from within herself.

Jesus' face seemed to become a bit brighter as he witnessed Aislinn's own energy increase. He smiled. "Your thoughts and emotions are transformative. As you focus on what aligns with the truth of the spiritual plane, you raise your own vibration and draw what matches your frequency to you. Your heart's energy draws to you what you need to continue on your journey—either toward or away from the creator."

The scene before them shifted. Instead of the mountain ridge, they were now in an urban park. There were two benches in front of them, not more than twenty meters apart. On the first sat a young woman with dark brown hair cropped close to her chin. Her face was downcast, and her eyes darted quickly from one point of focus to another, fearful, seeming to search for something. On the second bench rested a man in his late fifties, leaning slightly forward, feeding a flock of pigeons the crust from his recently finished sandwich. His eyes danced as he watched two rascally birds quarrel over a large piece of crust. The man mercifully tossed another piece to the loser of the scuffle. Two children drew near, watching the man and his birds with expressions of delight. The man handed his remaining strip of crust to the younger of the two kids, a girl with red hair gathered in feathery pig tails, about four years of age. She split the large strip as evenly as her small fingers could manage and passed one portion to her older brother. The pigeons scuttled over to the children, following their potential snack with great interest. The man leaned back and gently folded his arms, clearly entertained by the children's joy. Aislinn smiled, feeling the mutual positive aura from every being engaged with the man.

Jesus gestured toward the woman. She was observing the same scene, but instead of sharing in the warm feelings, her brow was furrowed, and she appeared irritated. The sound of the children shrieking with joy reached her ears. She stood, frowned slightly, and walked down the path, her back to the children.

"Did the children disturb her peace?" Aislinn asked.

"It appeared that way, but if she had genuinely been seeking to commune with nature and God, her expression and reaction would have differed. She may have sought a quieter place in the park with a smile and a nod to the children. What you saw goes much deeper. The young woman is filled with negative, self-focused, critical energy. She was unable to receive the flow of positive energy and joy from the others as their energy was not consistent with her own. She felt uncomfortable in their presence and turned away.

"The man's energy *was* very different," Aislinn observed. "He was overflowing with positive energy."

"Yes! And you saw what happened. The birds, the children—positive energy and emotions were drawn to him, as if to a magnet. What you experience on Earth has much to do with the energy you have within yourself. Those who give and receive love easily draw like-hearted beings to them. Their positive energy literally transforms their reality. Their physical health, the experiences that come to them—their external world will mirror what is within them. They even perceive the difficulties of life differently—through a lens of trust in their creator."[97]

This made sense to her. Aislinn felt this reality acutely in heaven. Whatever she thought of, asked for or focused on came into existence. She felt curiosity about the heavenly city and instantly found herself flying towards it. She expressed interest in life on other planets and experienced these planets firsthand. When she felt joy, her surroundings shared it with her, vibrating with a frequency similar to her own.[98] She marveled that the same was true on Earth—she would have a much greater impact on her Earthly experience than she had realized.

Aislinn remembered struggling with fear, doubt, and guilt, negativity coursing both through, and out of, her body. She realized now that those thoughts and emotions only brought more pain on herself. Stress upset her stomach and brought on headaches. A grumpy mood drove away those who usually brought her joy. When she returned to her physical body, she would need to be aware of what filled her mind and nourish those thoughts that would create both within and without the world she desired.

As she continued to watch the man and the children's joy, Aislinn's heart went out to the woman, who clearly was struggling more than Aislinn ever had. If Aislinn's thoughts and emotions so drastically affected her own experience of her life, what could be done for those drowning in that sort of negativity?

"What about those like that woman, who are filled with negative energy?" Aislinn asked. "Is there anything that can be done to help lift them from their downward spiral?"

Jesus smiled at her compassionate thought. Her heart was good, but she needed to remember that she was a small but valued part of something much larger than herself.

"Remember, you are like a farmer, gifted with the knowledge of how to plant the seeds of truth in the world. This is a knowledge that is not common. But you did not create the seeds. You also do not create the weather, and, in the end, the outcomes are outside of your control," Jesus reminded her. "You must surrender the ultimate outcome to the Father. All things are in his hands. Yet, your heart is good, and I know you yearn to do all that you can, and there is much that *is* within your power. Perhaps this will help."

In front of them, a large pond appeared, its banks surrounded by cattails and marsh grasses. A light breeze stirred the grasses and they rustled gently as Jesus and Aislinn moved past them to the edge of the water. Jesus leaned down and picked up a small grey stone situated on the edge of the bank. He handed it to Aislinn and gestured toward the water.[99]

"Here. Take this stone. Throw it as far as you can and watch what happens."

Aislinn took the small stone and tossed it into the water, already knowing what to expect, but not yet fully grasping the meaning. The stone hit the water with a soft splash, and she watched as ever-widening circles formed around the point of impact. Each circle extended further than the previous, the effect of the small splash reaching even the far edges of the pond. As she watched the ripples extend outward, the meaning became clear to her.

"Our actions have impacts far beyond what we expect," she said.

"Yes," Jesus replied, watching as the ripples slowly dissipated. "Whether for good or ill, not just our actions but also our words and even our thoughts have far-reaching effects on the souls of others. At best, we only notice the effects on those closest to us. But our actions go far beyond what we realize. Even the smallest kindness can be impactful. This lesson you saw first-hand during your life review with your grandfather, but it bore repeating."

Aislinn nodded and waited, knowing that there was more that Jesus wanted to share with her.

Jesus handed her two stones this time—one, another small grey rock, the other just a bit larger and more brown in color.

"This time, toss the small stone first," he said. "Imagine this is an action stemming from fear or anger. Watch the ripples."

Aislinn sent the stone on a beautiful arc through the air and watched as it landed with a gentle "plunk", ripples spreading from the point of impact.

"Now toss the larger stone so that it lands a few feet from the first," Jesus instructed. "This stone represents an action stemming from love, a subtler yet more powerful emotion."

She tossed in the larger stone as directed and watched as the rings created by the larger stone overpowered and began to cancel out the smaller stone's effects. Although the first stone's rings managed to reach one edge of the pond, the majority of its ripples were completely overcome by the ripples produced by the latter.

"Even one kind act stemming from a heart connected to God can overcome evil," Jesus explained. "It may take years, even lifetimes, but in almost all but the rarest cases, love will win in the end—it is the only thing that is true. Love is the strongest force in the universe."

13

Love the person in front of you

Back in the field, still in Jesus' company, Aislinn strolled down the path by the stream and soon found an ornate metallic bench that delighted her, designs of leaves and small birds etched into its frame. She eased her way onto the bench, allowing her light-form's feet to brush through the grass. She enjoyed feeling the texture, smell, and taste of the grass, the sweet flavor and the energy emitted by the plant filling her with joy. Jesus sat beside her, equally enjoying the experience and sharing that delight with Aislinn.

She felt increasingly ready to return. She dreaded no longer being enveloped and surrounded by the energy of the divine, but Jesus had given her the tools necessary for training her mind and opening her heart to the spiritual energy around her. Given time, she would be able to receive the guidance of the Spirit and feel the song of God within her being, even on the physical plane.

She realized that the knowledge she had received here of the true nature of God and the beauty of all there is had incomparable value. This was the treasure buried in a field that Jesus spoke of in one of his parables, the treasure worth selling all one's worldly possessions to buy.[100] Her heart went out to those who still were lost, as she once had been, forgetting their worth and purpose. Aislinn considered that perhaps she could bring some of the treasure she had discovered back to Earth and do her part to awaken others to their true nature. Something came alive inside her as she imagined the good she could do with this incredible gift.

Her heart shone brighter as she shared her dream with the Lord. "I want to devote the rest of my Earthly days to bringing your message, your truth, to others. What can I do?"

Jesus smiled gently, touched by Aislinn's bravery but knowing the enormity of what she was asking. "The answer is quite simple but will prove very hard in practice: Love the person in front of you. In everything you do, anywhere you go, simply love."[101]

Jesus' words gave her pause. Love, genuine love as she now understood it, had not come easily to Aislinn before. She hoped that knowing the reality and magnificence of existence as well as being anchored in a deep understanding of her own self-worth would make it possible.

"Yes, Aislinn. Knowing your worth is essential. Only by being rooted in the truth of your own value will you be able to honor the value of others. Thus, the first step to bringing a bit of heaven to Earth is to stay connected to the reality of who you are. As I have already taught you, take time regularly to step away from worldly distractions and allow God's love to fill you. In the mountains, you experienced the symphony of the divine inherent in nature. When you sit in meditation, you allow the notes of that same song to resonate within your being. You remember who you are. Then, as the music grows within you, as you allow the melody of the divine to play itself out in your life, others harmonize with you, joining in God's symphony."

Aislinn had intuitively understood while on the spiritual plane that energy was at the foundation of all life, of all creation. As souls became more like the creator, their vibration, a song of sorts, increased. Though Jesus' explanation was beautiful, it seemed very non-specific. Aislinn desired more concrete guidelines for loving, something akin to one of Jesus' famous sermons.

"Giving you specific instructions for how to handle any particular situation or relationship on Earth is futile," Jesus responded. "Once you are living in unity with the Spirit, once your soul is singing the truth of who you are, the particulars will fall into place. However, if you are out of tune, no amount of human effort to walk the walk will do. The change must come from within you."[102]

Jesus continued. "There is a difference between acting in love and being love. In the case of the former, you live from your mind, forming habits that, though virtuous, have no depth behind them and have little effect. However, once you are living in harmony with the Spirit, the waves of positive energy will emanate from you naturally. Though not all your actions will be flawless, other souls will feel the energy you emanate. They will recognize in you their own essence and their own value. You will be the presence of God in the lives of those around you."[103]

The distinction Jesus made was clear to Aislinn. However, even when she felt most at peace within herself, there were times when that feeling was eroded away by others' negativity.

"Often the negative energy from others makes it difficult for me to maintain my own positive spirit," Aislinn countered.

"Yes. Even when you are fully connected to the love both within and around you, you will daily meet with resistance from those who are lost or who do not know their own identity and treat you worse for it. This is why it is so important to spend time in connection with God, to allow the Spirit to fill your cup and guide your steps."

Aislinn thought about the ripples on the pond, the stronger ripples of love overpowering those whose origin was negative. Yet there were times that this rule seemed not to apply. Even when she was most grounded in her faith, there were situations when others' actions made it very difficult to offer love to them. Her uncle picked a fight with her over politics at every family gathering. She had a coworker or two who put forth the minimal effort to earn a paycheck, leaving dozens of students with a subpar education. How could she look past these clear offenses to God's spirit and love these people as Jesus was asking? She knew Jesus would have an answer—for every seeming problem that came to her mind, Jesus had a way to work through it. His ways were challenging but rooted in truth.

"What about the people who are clearly in the wrong and hurting others in the process? People like the Pharisees? How do you love them?" Aislinn asked.

"All souls are deserving of your love, Aislinn. See every person not for their words or actions, whether good or ill, but for who they are, even if they themselves have forgotten—sons and daughters of God."

"That's what you did while you were on Earth, wasn't it? Saw past the exterior of people and loved them for who they truly were?"

Jesus' eyes smiled, his heart contented with the ease that Aislinn could take on a new perspective.

"Yes, Aislinn. Where others saw a lifelong sinner, or a corrupted soul, I saw beloved children of God who had forgotten their identity and home. In this is the secret to forgiveness—seeing who beings truly are, not the masks they wear as they experience their lives on this plane."[104]

The corner of Aislinn's lip lifted a bit; she understood. "Father forgive them, for they know not what they do."[105]

Jesus nodded. "Regardless of their choices, their behavior, or their outward appearance, all souls have great worth. Seeing and treating these souls as the beautiful essence of the Creator that they are will remind them of what is true. At first, they may turn away, unable to accept that they are worthy of being regarded with such tenderness. But, given time and compassion from others on the physical and spiritual planes, a closed heart can be healed."

From their place on the bench, Jesus motioned for Aislinn to look outwards. In front of them, three windows appeared, each with a still frame image from Aislinn's earthly life.

"In addition to allowing the song of the divine to well up within you and seeing each person for who they are at their core," Jesus said, "understanding how your interactions with others aid in your own spiritual growth is also beneficial. Through your relationships, you come to know yourself better and receive instruction on how to love more deeply and wisely. When you are able to see the growth opportunities in your relationships with other souls, you are both able to maximize your soul's growth and see those interactions in a more positive light."[106]

In the window to the right, Aislinn saw an image of herself and Dave. They were sitting at the small kitchen table in Dave's home, eating spaghetti and talking over their day. Since their homes were within a couple miles of each other, many evenings during their engagement were spent sharing stories from their day over dinner. Dave's smiles and laughter would be a bright light to Aislinn, giving her a different perspective on the various struggles she had with her students and colleagues. He was a wonderful listener, allowing Aislinn to simply talk and let out her frustration when she needed to and providing advice when it was warranted. This night, however, Dave's brow was furrowed, and storms raged in his eyes as he shared with Aislinn how he had been passed over for a promotion.

"Do you remember this night?" Jesus asked.

"Yes. Dave vented for upwards of an hour about how he had been done wrong by his boss. It seemed like nothing I could say would lift his spirits. In his anger and frustration, he was so unpleasant to be near. I couldn't wait to be home and away from him."

Jesus smiled. "You even took off your engagement ring and threw it at the wall that night."

Aislinn realized that Jesus wasn't judging her, despite the sickening nature of her selfish behavior; rather, he was highlighting an important lesson.

"I wondered if I wanted to be married to a man who saw the world that way," Aislinn admitted. "My emotions were short-lived, luckily. Seeing it now, I know that my thinking was completely unfair to Dave. That was probably the one day in the entirety of our relationship that his mood was so sour."

Jesus turned on the bench to face Aislinn and looked at her intently, his gaze seeing through to her heart. "Why do you think this particular mood of Dave's bothered you so much?"

She was confused. Jesus gestured in front of them, smiling kindly.

Another image was displayed in the same window. Another night at the table, though this time she was seeing the room from Dave's perspective. This time, Aislinn was the one with the creased brow and look of consternation.

Seeing herself through Dave's eyes, she was instantly humbled. The behavior that had incited such anger from Aislinn was what Dave had to deal with in her almost daily. Yet Dave didn't seem to be bothered by her frequently negative outlook on life.

Jesus explained. "Often, the actions and words of others that evoke the greatest reaction in us are those areas in which we most need to grow. Responses tied to areas where we need little improvement tend to draw out a more compassionate response instead. For instance, your husband was rarely bothered by your negativity because it was something he had already overcome within himself. In this way, others are like mirrors that we look into to see the truth about ourselves."

Aislinn understood. "So, when I find myself reacting strongly to a situation, I should look for that same quality or behavior in myself?"

"Exactly. The more you are able to look inward and find the areas that need attention within yourself, the more your relationships can be a catalyst for your growth."

"Pulling the log out of my own eye before I remove the splinter from theirs."[107]

"Yes, Aislinn," Jesus affirmed. "You understand."

Her attention shifted to the second window. In this one, she saw her grandfather the day they practiced the two-step for the wedding, slowly and consciously preparing their snack. She remembered how much his purposeful movement had touched her and awakened in her the desire to have the same peace and sense of presence within herself.

"Here, your grandfather delivered a message. Just as you receive wisdom and guidance from guides and angels from the spiritual world, you also have earthly guides and teachers as well. Sometimes they are aware of their job. For instance, a parent is aware of their responsibility to provide direction and guidance for their children. These are guides who teach purposefully. However, at other times, the Holy Spirit, the spirit of the creator, uses the actions and choices of others to guide and provide direction, without the conscious knowledge of the teacher. Pop was a teacher and messenger for you. It was decided before your births that he would play this role in your life. In his advanced age he would be at a place in his journey where he could provide guidance to your struggling soul. At times, you were both aware of this; at others, the Spirit worked through him without either of your conscious knowledge."

"Though my grandfather was not a hard person to love, I could have learned even more than I did from his example," Aislinn said, considering the treasure trove of wisdom and experience that her interactions with Pop could have been, had she been even more open to learning from him.

"Yes," Jesus said. "You learn how to love and balance compassion with wisdom in part by watching others and learning from their example. Though you did not struggle to see the value of your relationship with your grandfather, there are other teachers who are not as obvious, and far more challenging to appreciate."

They shifted their gaze to the left to the scene in the final window. In the image, her uncle was questioning Aislinn's political leaning, espousing a view that Aislinn knew infringed on the rights of black Americans. Aislinn's chest tightened, and she tried to remain calm as she provided logical support for her opinion. Her uncle had little evidence to defend his position and began turning red, blood rushing to his face as his frustration at his perceived opponent escalated to anger. Despite Aislinn's calm mannerism, he became more heated and began calling her "young and ignorant". Aislinn indicated that she would be happy to talk to him further once he could treat her with respect and walked away calmly, determined to not let her uncle's taunts get to her.

She quickly caught on to Jesus' reason for sharing this moment. "In addition to honoring each person as a magnificent part of the creator, I also can learn by noticing those choices that do not align with who I am."

Jesus folded his hands on his lap and smiled. "Yes, Aislinn. Whether what you see is motivated by love or fear, from connection to the creator or separation from the divine, you can learn from each interaction the effects of a soul's choices. In addition, in every interaction there is the opportunity to practice integrating grace and wisdom under pressure. You did very well with your uncle that day. It was a beautiful learning opportunity for both of you."

Jesus took in their surroundings, taking in the magnificence and diversity of color and design of the plants, flowers, birds, and trees before them.

"By daily joining in the song of the creator, the music within you will naturally overflow and transform the hearts of others," he said. "In any moment, you can become more practiced at seeing through to the essence and true worth of the person before you, and the learning opportunities inherent in each interaction, spreading the truth of the kingdom." He stood from the bench and looked back at Aislinn. "And you are not alone—countless others in connection with the Spirit seize every moment as an opportunity to enter more fully into the kingdom of heaven. Together, you will bring that kingdom to Earth."

14

The Future

"I know you are far wiser than I, but I cannot see how your plan for bringing the kingdom to Earth will work," Aislinn admitted.

As far as Aislinn knew, there always had been, and, she assumed, always would be a large amount of evil on Earth. The quality of life on Earth was unraveling quickly. Humanity now had the technology to annihilate full regions of the globe, the climate was in crisis, natural disasters were increasing in frequency, and division and conflict born of power-hungry leaders and their self-seeking constituents were rampant, regardless of culture. Jesus' simple plan seemed insufficient to take on the magnitude of the difficulty Aislinn foresaw for her Earthly home.

Jesus' face became more serious than Aislinn's. His eyes held hers, gentle and steady.

"There is immense power in one soul valuing another. How many souls do you interact with each day?"

Aislinn considered this. As a teacher, she interacted with almost two hundred souls daily. She taught more than one hundred students, and then interacted with faculty, friends, family, neighbors, and countless strangers in her comings and goings.

"What if you saw them, truly saw them? Loved them for who they are? And what if even a small percentage of those souls are then inspired to do the same?"

Jesus paused, letting Aislinn consider this. "We will not let humanity destroy themselves and their planet. You are an integral part of the plan. I told you earlier that there was more than one reason you were here on the spiritual plane. The first reason was for your own healing. The second was to help in this mission. Your heart and will are strong, Aislinn, and, equipped with what you will remember from your time here, you will impact the lives of many, awakening them to their true selves."

Jesus' compassion for humanity was palpable. "It will work, Aislinn. Love—one soul to another—is the only thing that ever has." [108]

Jesus' eyes showed sadness. "Yet even with this plan, souls on Earth will experience great upheaval. Just as each individual soul learns from the consequences of their choices on Earth, humanity at large must learn from their shared choices. Your planet will soon undergo major changes as a result of the collective conscience of the souls living there. There is a chance this can be avoided, if beings on Earth can significantly change without such a forceful teaching of the consequences of their actions."

Aislinn's conscience was filled with visions of the future Earth, the planet undergoing extreme upheaval. Hurricanes, earthquakes, floods, and volcanic eruptions covered the Earth, occurring with a frequency that was unprecedented. She witnessed the levels of the ocean rising and countless souls suffering. Sadness overwhelmed her as she witnessed all of this, feeling the pain of the beings on Earth as they struggled for survival in the midst of chaos.[109]

Jesus' presence was calming, overpowering the heartbreak she felt witnessing the widespread disaster. "You must be strong and trust in our plan, no matter how bleak conditions on Earth become. Continue to be love to those in your life and be patient. We are working through you and others to bring something beautiful to fruition. The only way change is possible is through changing the inner being of one person at a time. Wars and disasters happen because your collective conscience desires dominance over others strongly. Times of extreme turmoil may be necessary for humanity at large to experience a shift in their spiritual energy. Through the power of love from one person to another, and, if needed, the natural consequences of humanity's choices, there *will be* a change in the overall consciousness of the souls on Earth. Within the next two centuries, your world will become almost unrecognizable.[110]

Jesus transported them to what Aislinn understood intuitively to be Earth, though it did not resemble the Earth that she knew.[111] The scene before her was reminiscent of a Native American community with characteristics of the Garden of Eden. Humans coexisted peacefully with both the environment and the creatures within it, as well as with each other. The people's garments were simple, with limited decoration and minimal jewelry. The community Aislinn witnessed was close knit, with people of all ages collaborating in the day's activities. An older woman was teaching a young boy about growing vegetables while a middle-aged man played a game of tag with a group of young children. A handful of adults in their twenties danced and played music together. The focus for many of them was the children, the adults visibly enjoying their time with them and putting great effort into teaching them about compassion and the wonders of their natural world. Work appeared to be play for the community and their every move part of a dance of love for their creator, themselves, and each other. They seemed to have joined in the model of giving and receiving that was inherent in nature.

"Does all humanity live in this way, or just in this place?" Aislinn asked.

"All humanity will live in small communities, like this one. However, each has its own identity and culture," Jesus answered. "The music enjoyed, language spoken, and what the people seek to learn through their time on Earth is unique to each."

Again, Aislinn saw that experiences both on the spiritual and physical planes, even on this rejuvenated Earth, seemed tailored to celebrate the uniqueness of the individual.

She marveled at how free of conflict and negativity this community seemed to be. This seemed incongruous with what she understood about the purpose of Earth.

"Collectively, souls on Earth have grown beyond needing the degree of separation from the divine that you currently experience," Jesus explained. "And, if a soul still needs separation to grow, other planets are available for them to mature at the pace that is right for them."

As Aislinn continued to enjoy and marvel at the community, she noticed a man lying on a mat, with a half dozen others surrounding him. The man looked unwell, but peaceful. Those gathered around him were laying their hands on him, their eyes closed in concentration.

"What are they doing?" Aislinn asked.

"They are healing him through prayer and the exchange of energy."

Aislinn connected this form of healing with what Jesus had just explained about the more advanced nature of the souls in these communities.

"This form of healing—is this the result of the higher energy level of souls on Earth?"

"With the right energy within it, the human body as you currently know it can harness these abilities," Jesus answered. "However, the human form is also slowly evolving over time, making access to spiritual energy easier. The largest changes, however, will not be in the human body, but rather in the ratio of loving energy and its opposite on Earth. As you have witnessed here, many of the woes of your current society will disappear as humanity evolves. There will be no war or violence and almost all interactions will be loving. However, people will occasionally fall ill, some physically, others spiritually. Regardless of what is causing the disease, the community does what it can to help that soul return to health. In the case of physical illness, humans will use prayer, touch, and meditation. If the illness is primarily spiritual or if solitude is more beneficial for the soul, the community will support the person in spending time alone to heal and surround them only with prayer and guidance."

"If sickness is so easily healed, do they only die of old age?"

Jesus gestured towards a group of elderly members of the community. "People can live as long as they would like. However, souls choose to move on from their experience once they have accomplished all that they seek to in their lifetime. They simply lie down when they are ready to return to the spiritual plane, and their spirit moves on. They are surrounded by their loved ones as they pass from their bodies. Death is a time of rejoicing for the community."

"So, death isn't feared?"

Jesus nodded. "Every part of the soul's journey is embraced. Each soul is here to grow in holiness, but this planet and any single lifetime on Earth can only teach so much. At a certain point, it is best for souls to return to their spirit forms and choose a different experience to help in their continued evolution. Others in the community celebrate this as a graduation of sorts. They rejoice in the unique opportunity to celebrate the growth in maturity and beauty of the soul."

Aislinn thought of how differently she had viewed death on Earth—as something horrible, tragic, to be dreaded even. She had never considered it a blessing and something to rejoice in.

As she quietly watched the community, a couple farming the land captured her attention. Their hands hovered lovingly over the soil, and they looked to be at peace. As she watched, a head of lettuce sprouted and developed into its mature form within minutes, something that would be impossible on the current Earth. Aislinn turned to Jesus in disbelief.

"How is this possible?"

"When I was on Earth, I told you that you could move a mountain into the sea with the power of faith.[112] One day soon, beings on Earth will evolve to the point that they will learn how to harness this creative power. The same power that is used in the healing of illnesses in these communities will be used to grow food—the power of love and the interconnectedness with all things."

"Why not teach us this gift centuries ago? Why wait for us to nearly destroy the Earth?"

"All wisdom and abilities, from the harnessing of the power of fire to the knowledge of the energy within an atom were given when souls on Earth have sufficiently evolved to use the knowledge primarily for the good of themselves and others. Even still, you see how these gifts have been misused."[113]

Images of the bombings of Nagasaki and Hiroshima came to her mind. Even the process of testing the atomic bomb cost unconscionable destruction to nature and human life.

"The method of harnessing energy that is being used to heal the body and to grow food is much greater than anything humanity has been graced with to date," Jesus explained. "It has immense power for good. Already, humanity has developed a basic understanding of the power of unseen forces of energy. Research has shown the influence of music on plant growth, positive interactions with other humans and animals on overall wellbeing, and prayer on physical healing.[114] This understanding will grow and deepen over the coming decades. With these newfound abilities, all humans will have the ability to communicate telepathically with each other and with members of other communities around the world. In addition, with these same abilities, control of the weather through the mind and communication with beings on other planets across vast distances in the same manner will be possible. But beings on Earth need to mature before they can safely use these gifts."

This made sense to her. Already, humans had used the ease of wireless communication for harm, to manipulate and emotionally injure others. She could imagine the gift of telepathy being used in a more extreme fashion to break down people, perhaps even control others, denying them their human freedom. In the wrong hands, such great power could be used for unspeakable destruction.

"As humanity grows in connection to God and one another, we will teach you how to harness these hidden abilities. When you return, you will help your brothers and sisters to grow in that love and connection. As you grow as a collective, you will make possible the coming of this new Earth."

As Aislinn looked over the beautiful scene before her, she knew she strongly desired this life for her grandchildren and great-grandchildren. It was an honor to be able to return and play a role, no matter how small, in bringing this miracle-filled living, this new Earth, into being.

15

The Return

The vision of the Earth faded. Jesus and Aislinn were immersed in a peaceful darkness. Aislinn kept her eyes fixed on Jesus, knowing already what was to come.

"It is time, Aislinn. You will never feel completely ready, but there is nothing else I can do here to prepare you for the transition back."

Even though she was committed to her decision and Jesus had answered every question that she had about the return, she still felt a wave of fear and resistance.

Jesus was loving but firm. "I will go with you. I will never leave you alone, dear one."

Like a young child clinging to her mother's leg, Aislinn soul clung to Jesus, soaking in every second of his loving presence. They flew together, and soon they were hovering above the still form of her body on the beach. A man with long light brown hair pulled back in a bun was pressing firmly on her chest with two hands. Dave stood nearby with another medic beside him.

"Please, Aislinn, please," Dave begged. "Just one breath, I know you can do this." The man put his mouth to the barrier laying across her lifeless lips and exhaled twice. Aislinn watched her body's chest rise with the influx of air. He began pressing hard on her chest again. Jesus changed Aislinn's perspective, moving her spirit form to the front of her body so that Dave's face would be her focus. His eyes were wide and panicked, red and swollen in his grief. Tears streamed down his cheeks. Aislinn's heart went out to him. Her love for her husband filled her and she instinctively reached for him to comfort him. As she moved toward him, her spirit slipped back into her physical form.

Back in her body, Aislinn gasped for air, her eyes wide open, her lungs screaming in agony.[115]

"Stay with me Aislinn, just stay with me," Dave pleaded. His eyes met hers, a mix of intense love and fear, thrilled to have her alive but afraid for her to lose consciousness again. Aislinn wretched, large amounts of fluid clearing from her body. Her lungs were in extraordinary pain, forcing her to grimace and close her eyes again. When she opened them, Dave was looking at someone or something behind her. She heard the voices of two men, different from her rescuers. Distracted by her pain, she was unable to catch every word, but got the gist of the conversation. There was an ambulance just in front of their hotel, and these two men were going to carry her to it.

Aislinn felt two strong pairs of arms supporting her neck, back, and legs, lifting her gently from the sand onto a stretcher. As her body was being moved, she could hear Dave thanking the fire department rescuers who had gotten her this far. The stretcher rose; Aislinn looked into the eyes of those carrying her and was stunned at the kindness and love that shone through them. The men were tall, surprisingly so, one with olive skin, the other ebony in color. Her chest was still screaming in pain, but the kindness in their gaze was soothing. Dave, who was keeping pace beside them, even looked calmer.

Eventually they reached the front of their hotel and, as promised, an ambulance was waiting. The tall emergency workers placed her gently in the back of the ambulance. Before leaving, the darker skinned man placed his strong right hand gently on Aislinn's chest, the other on her head. Though an unusual action from a stranger, Aislinn trusted him and closed her eyes, her body exhausted and still in incomprehensible pain. As she relaxed, Aislinn felt power coursing from the man's hand through her chest. The pain in her lungs immediately subsided. Aislinn opened her eyes and gazed up in wonder at the man hovering over her, looking on her with great love. These were no ordinary men. Aislinn smiled in gratitude to her angels, who simply nodded in response.[116] She turned her head to check on Dave, finally able to give him the attention that before now had been devoted to managing the pain of her tortured body. Dave smiled, relieved to see her face free of pain, then turned to thank the men.

But when Dave lifted his head, they had vanished. He turned to Aislinn in disbelief.

"What just happened?"

"They're gone," she answered.

"Two seven-foot-tall men don't just disappear like that," Dave argued, trying to come to terms with what he had just witnessed.

"I don't think they were men, Dave." Aislinn coughed, her chest still sore, but no longer agonizingly so.

As the ambulance doors closed and they traveled to the hospital, Dave held Aislinn's hand tightly between his own. He bowed his head, closed his eyes, and said a silent prayer of gratitude, his dark hair falling across his forehead. Aislinn looked over at him, feeling great compassion and love for her husband.

She had barely returned to Earth and Jesus had already kept his promise. What she assumed were angels had been there for her and Dave in their moment of greatest need. She closed her eyes and said her own prayer of thanksgiving. The angels had given Aislinn two beautiful blessings: physical healing, and, just as important, proof of her journey. Now Dave would have more than just her word to go on. He, too, was witness to a miracle.[117]

_16_

Homesick

When they arrived at the hospital, several medical professionals descended upon Aislinn, having received word of the dire situation. She was quickly put on oxygen and connected to an array of monitors. Hours later, once Aislinn was given the details, she understood the reason for the hasty action of the doctors as well as the look of pure terror in Dave's eyes in the moments before her return. She had been swept out into the ocean's current fifteen minutes after sunrise, about 7:15 AM. Her surfing friends had called in for help immediately, but it was fifteen minutes before fire department rescue swimmers were able to pull her body to shore, and five minutes more before CPR was successful. Aislinn had been 'dead' for twenty minutes. Her chances of resuscitation had been slim, and, having been successfully resuscitated, the chances of her not incurring brain damage or heart failure within the next 48 hours were next to zero.[118]

She was not afraid. She knew that she would not have been sent back to Earth to become a vegetable or to die again, and the smile on Dave's face comforted her. However, leaving the warmth and love of heaven was even more difficult than she had expected. No longer surrounded by God's love, the Earth felt cold and lonely by comparison. The blandness of her cream-colored hospital room, even the dark blue of the curtains seemed so empty of the vibrance of heaven. However, she also noticed little things that she hadn't before her experience. Aislinn felt energy flow from Dave's hands when he touched her arm. She noticed a slight glow coming from everything around her, like a diminished version of what she had experienced on the other side of eternity. Yet even these reminders seemed to make her homesickness worse, reminding her of all that she had left behind.[119]

At the Edge of the Jordan

At 8 PM, Aislinn eyes moved between the clock and Dave. Visiting hours ended soon. She found Dave's presence comforting, his warm hand in hers and his smiling eyes making everything okay. However, she was confident that the couch didn't provide near the quality of sleep that their hotel room would, and she would be alright here overnight. Dave couldn't help but be worried for her physical health—almost no one in her position survived, and those few who did had irreparable damage to major organs. Aislinn knew she was the exception, but how could she explain this to her frightened husband?

Dave shuffled back from the window—the view of the street below offered little to interest him—and sat in the chair beside Aislinn's bed. He took Aislinn's hand in his and looked deep into her eyes.

"Everything's going to be okay," he said, more to reassure himself than her.

Aislinn smiled. "I'm going to be fine. They'll let me out of here soon enough and we can enjoy the rest of our honeymoon."

Dave looked at her as if the brain damage the doctors had warned him about was showing. A tall female pulmonologist had pulled him aside just after lunch and told him that today and tonight would be telling. There were no guarantees. Even though her vital signs and chest scans looked promising on intake, the doctor cautioned being overly optimistic under the circumstances. "We will do everything we can," she had promised.

Dave had spent the next fifteen minutes in one of the public areas with a box of hospital tissues trying to pull himself back together for his wife. He berated himself for being so stupid as to let Aislinn go out into the ocean without him and knew he would struggle to forgive himself. Then there was the potential of Aislinn being permanently physically and mentally disabled. Dave knew he would never leave his wife, but a life of being a caretaker was not at all what he had expected when they exchanged vows. And the thought of losing her completely was something he couldn't wrap his head around. He knew he needed to be strong, to help keep Aislinn's spirits high.

"You'll be out of here in no time, I'm sure," Dave lied, wishing he believed it.

Aislinn looked at the clock again—the window was closing for guests to leave. She got up the courage to speak again—though the pain was a shadow of what she felt immediately after her transition, talking still hurt, as did taking deep breaths.

"Sweetheart, go back and rest tonight. I'll be okay."

"No chance, Aislinn. I'm not leaving you. You can't get rid of me." Dave did his best to make his words sound like a challenge, his eyebrows lowered and a spark in his eyes to convey that he meant it.

Aislinn was too weary to fight him on this. She understood his fear and would do the same if their roles were reversed. She was also grateful to have him here, a reminder of why she had chosen to return.

A few hours later, Dave was asleep on the couch, having finally succumbed to the emotional exhaustion of the day. Alone for the first time since that morning, Aislinn felt a wave of sadness wash over her. But instead of giving into it, she turned to the wisdom that Jesus had previously relayed to her. She closed her eyes, slowed her breathing, and focused on the energy within her. At first, thoughts and emotions rushed through her, a torrent of sadness and frustration, mixed with gratitude and hope. She allowed her emotions to be as they were and went deeper. Over the minutes that followed the peaks of her emotional waves flattened and a calm came over her. Slowly, a feeling of peace overpowered her anxious heart, not as intense a peace as what she felt on the spiritual plane, but refuge enough from the emotional turmoil of her transition. Aislinn's spirit rested in that place within her, soaking in the joy of connection to the divine and the assurance that everything was in the hands of a power greater than herself. She drifted off to sleep happy.

Dave stayed by her side for her two-day stay in the hospital. Each day, her physical and emotional pain eased. She was able to laugh and joke with Dave. By the end of the second day, she felt physically well. Although she showed no signs of permanent organ damage, the medical professionals waited the full 48 hours to make sure that all was well before discharging her. Dave, not yet knowing about Aislinn's experience during those twenty minutes, gradually relaxed as the doctors' prognoses improved and Aislinn became more of her spunky self. On the morning of the third day, she was given the all clear by the hospitalist. After being handed the discharge papers, Dave smiled the first relaxed, happy smile Aislinn had seen since the accident. He leaned over the bed and kissed her. "We still have a couple days left of our honeymoon. How about we go and enjoy it?"

Seeing him so happy lifted Aislinn's spirits. She made a motion to rise from the hospital bed to dress. Dave's voice interrupted her.

"But Aislinn?"

"Yeah?"

"Let's take a break from surfing."

The first night back at the hotel was rough for the newlyweds. Aislinn found sleep elusive; her brain was still working overtime to process the last few days. Dave, understandably, was focused on Aislinn's breathing. Any change in pace or depth immediately raised an alarm. He was also trying to come to terms with the changes he noticed in Aislinn over the past couple of days. She looked like the Aislinn whose hand had been given to him a mere week before. Yet there was something different about her that he couldn't quite name. Instead of the spunky, ever-busy young woman he married, she was now calm and relaxed, almost aloof. That afternoon, their first after her discharge from the hospital, she was strangely content to just sit on the beach and stare at the waves rolling in and out, digging her feet into the sand and enjoying the rough texture of the grains between her toes. Dave naturally wanted his wife to be happy, but this new calm worried him. Was her brain altered or damaged in a way that the doctors didn't catch? Her memory was sharp and her conversations intelligent and thoughtful, but something didn't feel quite right.[120]

Come morning, both lay in bed, pretending to sleep. It was the final morning of their honeymoon as they were set to fly home to North Carolina later that day. At around seven, Aislinn decided more sleep wasn't happening and that a morning walk on the beach would be a better use of her time. Dave was eager to try out a nice restaurant for breakfast to celebrate the last morning of their honeymoon. They had reservations at 8:30, giving her enough time for a walk on the beach. She'd be sure to wear her watch though, just in case. She rose and changed into her sweat clothes. The beach was shockingly chilly in the mornings, before the marine layer had burned off.

"Dave," she said, seeing him stirring as she pulled her hair back into a ponytail, "Is it okay if I go out for a walk? I'll be sure to be back by eight."

Dave had no desire to be apart from her but understood that she might need the space.

"Okay," he said, a hint of reservation in his voice. "But take your phone with you, just in case."

Aislinn unplugged her phone from the charger and stashed it in the pocket of her sweatpants. She could tell Dave was nervous about her going out alone and appreciated his willingness to give her the opportunity to think and enjoy the ocean.

Once she reached the beach, Aislinn turned north, not wanting to return to the same swath where the incident occurred. The morning was beautiful. The sun warmed her skin, and the breeze was just enough to cool her skin. She became quickly caught up in watching the small brown plovers running in and out of the water, chased by the incoming tide. Aislinn marveled at how she now felt connected with each one of them, even with the water itself. This connectedness was less intense than what she had experienced in her soul-state, yet much stronger than anything she had felt on Earth prior.

She walked for several minutes, eventually reaching Huntington's famous pier. She had walked here with Dave one evening earlier in the week, enjoying the sunset over the water. She walked out on the pier a bit, stopping right where the waves crashed onto the shore. Here she could enjoy the fishermen on her left and the already bustling beach to her right. The sun had all but gotten rid of the thick fog and had visitors reaching for their sunscreen. A handful of beach volleyball enthusiasts were well into an early morning game up by the promenade. They were quite skilled, with multiple players making impressive diving saves and kill shots. Nearby, a young man was sitting on the sand, watching the game. One of the players spotted him and quickly invited him to join. Aislinn was too far away to be able to hear the exchange, but from what she could observe, the borderline professionals weren't taking no for an answer. Eventually, he joined in. He was lacking in skill, especially in comparison to the regulars. Yet he was clearly viewed as one of the group, his teammates cheering him on. Aislinn recognized the parallels between the dynamic of this simple volleyball game and what she had seen on the spiritual plane. These men and women cared far more about enjoying the game and developing their skills than about any score they may have been keeping in their heads. The concern for the group overshadowed any self-interest. She filed the memory away, proof that the type of community she had witnessed in heaven was possible here on Earth as well.

After a couple minutes of enjoying the dynamics of the volleyball game and the relaxing sound of the waves directly below her, Aislinn thought to look down to check the time—7:25. She found that difficult to believe, but assumed that perhaps, in addition to feeling more connected to nature, she was experiencing the flow of time differently now. She watched a few more points, impressed with the skill of the locals. The teams were hilariously unbalanced with the new addition, and yet no one seemed to care, including the man who was the "weak link". His face looked confident and proud. She made a mental note to try her hand at a game next time they came out to CA. Aislinn glanced down at her watch again, but the minute hand had still not moved—her watch had stopped. She was confused by this. The watch had never failed her before, and the batteries were not old. She reached into her pocket to fish out the cell phone. The phone would not turn on, though Aislinn was certain she had charged it the night before. Flummoxed and unsure of the correct time, she thought it wise to jog back to Dave, being mindful not to overtax herself, just to be sure they would make their breakfast date. As she made her way back to the hotel, she enjoyed the sounds of the ocean and the feeling of her feet on the sand. She felt no anxiety, a dramatic change from her former self. She intuitively realized what was important. Dave mattered, but she was doing her best to respect and care for him at that moment, so she could simply let any other worries go. She found herself enjoying the return trip--the rhythm of her heartbeat, the gentle rise and fall of her stomach as she breathed, and the wet sand beneath her feet. She was present—here and now. It was so beautiful, so freeing.[121]

When Aislinn opened the door to their room, Dave had an anxious look on his face. She wondered what time it was, if she had made them late for their date or if he was just on edge, this being their first time apart since the accident. She looked at the kitchen clock and saw that it was 8:15—fifteen minutes after she promised to be back. Her heart reached out to him in compassion for what must have been several minutes of panic. However, her calm refused to make way for guilt. As Jesus had taught her, when her heart was rooted in love, she would be able to respond in the way that would be most beneficial. In this case, it was calm compassion, not guilt, that would bring healing.

"I'm sorry, Dave," she said calmly, her eyes locked with his. "For some reason my watch stopped, and the phone is dead, even though I charged it last night. I lost track of time, sweetheart."

She could see the lingering concern in his expression. "I'm sorry for any anxiety I caused you. Are you still up for going to breakfast?"

Dave hugged her tightly, absorbing her peace and calm. "I think we'll be right on time if you can get dressed quickly."

They arrived at a beautiful, western-facing, oceanfront restaurant. As they entered the dining venue and neared the balcony, Dave put one hand over her eyes.

"I have a small surprise for you," he said. Aislinn loved the feeling of his hand against her face, his chest pressed against her back as they slowly stepped forward. She could feel his warm breath close to her ear. She marveled at how much more aware she was of everything. Her heightened appreciation of all that surrounded her, intense focus on the present moment, and awareness of the divine within all amplified her joy in even the smallest of actions. Several steps later, Dave stopped and slowly drew his hand back. They had the outdoor eating area all to themselves. There was a beautiful table set for just the two of them, with a simple bouquet of red and white roses at the center of the glass-topped table. One wrought iron chair was located on each side. The waiter slowly pulled out the one on the right for Aislinn, the napkin for her place setting in his hand.

"Dave, this is perfect!" Aislinn exclaimed, meeting the eyes of their waiter and smiling, then taking the seat offered.

"I figured if we were to have a shortened honeymoon, we might as well maximize the time we have together. With breakfast being your favorite meal and your love of nature, this seemed like the perfect fit."

Aislinn was touched by his thoughtfulness.

Dave looked at her calmly but intently. Aislinn could feel his eyes searching her mind and heart. He could already see and feel the difference in her but couldn't explain the reason for it. The depth and intensity of her gaze when she looked at him these last three days set his heart on fire. He had never received such love and raptured attention from her in the past. Yet, when Aislinn had taken her seat and thanked their waiter—a handsome, tall, blond-haired young man in his upper-twenties—he had seen the same intense expression in her eyes. Her loving focus was not exclusive to him.[122]

The waiter placed the cloth napkin on Aislinn's lap, poured them each a glass of water, and then left them to their menus. After making their selections, they had some time to themselves.

Dave reached across the table with his left hand, gently laying his wedding band over hers. His ring was broad, a wide gold band with a braided design. Aislinn's wedding ring was much thinner, more elegant, but its braided pattern matched Dave's. Just above the wedding band was Aislinn's engagement ring, a single small but sparkling diamond. Dave had researched the diamond thoroughly, getting the best quality, most brilliant stone he could afford. The week before proposing, he would sit on his patio and hold the ring in his hand, watching as the sunlight reflected off its facets, imagining the gorgeous ring on his soon-to-be fiancée's hand. He looked up from the rings to his wife's face, his expression a strange mix of deep happiness and concern.

"Aislinn, I don't know the best way to word this." He looked away briefly, then turned back to her, tapping his foot nervously. "What happened out there in the waves, before I found you?"

"Do you mean, what happened when I died?"

Dave was visibly unsettled.

"It's just that...well, whatever happened out there changed you, but I can't wrap my head around it. I would have thought that sort of trauma would have made you more nervous, or scared...sullen even. But instead, you're peaceful and radiant. It's not a bad thing at all, sweetheart, but you're just, I don't know...different."

Aislinn closed her eyes and smiled, saying a silent prayer of gratitude for this open door. With an opportunity to finally share what had consumed her since the moment of her return, it all came pouring out.

"It's real, Dave. Jesus, heaven, angels...it's all true..." Aislinn paused briefly. "I know it will take a lot of time for both of us to process this, but I feel strongly that what I experienced—fantastic though it may sound—was true."

Dave was still stuck on the first few words. "You SAW Jesus?" he asked.

Aislinn nodded, smiling broadly.

Aislinn shared everything that she could remember from her experience, Dave listening, so absorbed in her story that he didn't notice when his steak omelet was placed in front of him. Aislinn ended by relaying her memory of Dave's prayer on the beach, his crying out to her, and her return to her body. She took a deep breath and held it, hoping and praying that her words had reached a receptive audience.

Dave simply stared back, his jaw slightly open, his eyes wide. "I don't know what to say."

Aislinn's face fell, and she played with her hair, her eyes focused on the curled ends. "You don't believe me...that's okay, I didn't expect you to."

Dave tried to cover up his disbelief. "No, no...that's not it. I do believe you, Aislinn. At least, I think I do. It is all just so far beyond anything I could have guessed. It's a bit of a shock."

"I know. It's a bit overwhelming for me too. Although I was only out of my body for a few minutes in Earth time, I experienced enough to fill a lifetime."

Dave paused, over-whelmed and still wrapped up in his own thoughts. "Those men...the ones who helped get you to the ambulance, do you think they were angels?"

Aislinn bit her lip. "I'm not sure how to answer that yet. The angels on the spiritual plane did not look like people. They were far more radiant. If those 'men' were angels, which does make sense to me, then they must have altered their appearance so as not to concern us. But, angels or not, they healed me. Before they laid their hands on my chest, the pain of breathing was unbearable."

Dave nodded and took a deep breath, leaning back with a sigh, his fork tapping the table lightly as he gathered his thoughts.

"Your story explains a lot of what I've noticed about you...your peacefulness, and the way you interact with everyone we come across, as if each one were someone very important to you." He leaned forward again, his usual calm returning. "You're different, but I love who you've become."

'So...you don't regret what happened?"

Dave paused, choosing his words carefully. "Aislinn, I will struggle for some time with forgiving myself for not being out there on the beach with you that morning. But, as for what came of it...well, you're alive, filled with joy, and we have a lifetime of memories before us. I'm grateful."

17

Faith

The wrench clattered to the floor of the kitchen. The top-of-the-line dishwasher Dave had purchased just over a year before was now refusing to drain, dirty dish water pooling at its base. He had cleared the line, reconnected the electric, and started up the drain cycle...nothing. Dave sighed loudly and walked to the living room, plopping on the couch. Aislinn was sitting on the far end, her feet propped up on the ottoman, their rather obese gray tabby curled up by her side, tilting his chin to just the right angle so that her fingers scratched the bottom perfectly. Aislinn was gazing out the window at the tree line in the distance, taking in the beauty of the view. She looked over at Dave and smiled, love and contentment in her eyes. He tossed an uneasy grin back her way, swallowing his temporary frustration.

There had been an uneasy peace between them since their return home to North Carolina. Something Dave couldn't understand or fully believe had happened on the beach that morning a few weeks before, something that had taken a part of his wife away from him. This Aislinn was completely different from the spirited emotional rollercoaster of a woman whom he had proposed to months before. Her level of calm now eclipsed his own. He was unsettled, struggling to find his role in the altered relationship. Aislinn knew the drastic change in her was hard on her husband. She was confident that they would weather this transition, that their deep devotion to each other would pull them through.

"I'm sorry, Dave. I guess the dishwasher is still out of commission?" Aislinn asked compassionately, acutely aware of but unfazed by his obvious anxiety.

"Damn thing is beyond my basic level of mechanical skill. I can't believe I spent a full paycheck on that piece of garbage just to have it die one week after it goes out of warranty."

"I really appreciate you trying to fix it and wish I knew something more about appliances so I could help. Even if we can't fix it though, I'm sure we can find a new, less expensive model." Aislinn kept her eyes locked on his, clearly feeling his emotion but not reflecting his inner turmoil. She could have been back on the beach, the level of peace on her face. For some reason, this only made him more anxious.

"With the hospital bills coming in, our portion of the wedding expenses, and the holidays around the corner, we simply can't afford a new dishwasher right now." Dave watched Aislinn's face...no reaction. The old Aislinn would be up in arms with him for throwing the hospital bills into the discussion. He admitted it was a jerk move, a product of his deep levels of pent-up frustration.

"We'll figure something out, Dave. And I'll take care of the dishes in the sink once this pile of fluff decides he's had enough attention." Aislinn turned her gaze downwards to the purring mound of gray still nestled in close to her. Toby was her cat and moved in along with Aislinn. Dave was more of a dog person but tolerated cats well-enough. His relationship with her cat had started off strained when Toby, upon entering Dave's house for the first time, had marked his territory on his freshly laundered dress shirts. After the rocky start, the two of them got along fairly well.

"Pile of lazy fat's more like it," Dave retorted. In his heart he was begging Aislinn to react, to get into the verbal back and forth that he secretly enjoyed, even to need him to calm her, like she used to. He would gladly welcome an argument to reassure him that the woman he knew was still in there.

"Yeah, maybe we should feed him a little less." Aislinn smiled at Dave again, clearly not bothered by his passive aggressive remark.

Dave felt a mix of anger and despair wash over him. He was in disbelief over his behavior. He had a beautiful, happy, healthy wife who loved him, and here he was trying to pick a fight with her—anything to bring back what was safe and familiar. She didn't deserve this from him, and he hated himself for being this way. He knew he needed to get away and reset, to figure himself out.

"I'm going to go out for a drive for a bit to clear my head," he said. "You need anything?"

"Nothing for now; thanks for asking though." Aislinn gently shifted Toby to the side. She walked over to Dave and embraced him. She pulled back and looked at him, wishing she could ease the turmoil within him.

"Try the church next to the bakery downtown," she suggested. "The sunlight looks beautiful pouring through the stained glass this time of day."

Dave raised an eyebrow. This wasn't the first time Aislinn had seemed to know what he was feeling or what he needed without him saying a word. It was as if she heard his thoughts instead of his words. There was no hiding anything from her—yet another of the many things that unnerved him.[123]

"Not a bad idea," he said, reaching for his hoodie. Knowing she understood what he was feeling calmed him. He turned around and looked at her, genuinely grateful for her kindness. "Thanks, Aislinn."

Dave arrived at the church around 5 PM. It was Sunday evening, and the church lot was empty. The late autumn sun was low in the sky. Aislinn was right—the sunlight would be beautiful as it poured through the stained glass inside. Apart from their wedding, he hadn't set foot in a church in years.

Over the past few weeks, he had spent many sleepless nights wrestling with the changes he had seen in Aislinn. For one thing, all her constant fidgeting and worrying were completely absent. She exuded calm regardless of the circumstance. The only emotion besides her ever-present quiet peace were the occasional moments of sadness that would overcome her—usually at night. These weren't the worried tears when her grandfather was sick or even the tears of grief following Pop's death. These tears were different, and he couldn't understand them. He wondered if she was secretly unhappy in their marriage and that it all came out as she tried to sleep. Once he had worked up the nerve to put his arm around her as she cried. She had quietly whispered "thank you", her sobs turning to soft hiccups as she calmed in his embrace. But most nights he pretended to be asleep, afraid of what she might reveal if he asked her what was wrong, afraid that there was something wrong with her that he couldn't fix, that the accident had harmed her, or, even worse, that he was the cause of her pain.

His hand gripped the large brass handle and the door creaked open. He walked to the middle right of the church, the sound of his footsteps reverberating off the wood rafters, and slowly sat down in a pew. He leaned back and took in the beauty of the blue, red, and gold light that filled the sanctuary as the scenes from the New Testament seemed to come to life before him. To the right and left of center, the setting sun illuminated images of angels, the halos above their heads a brilliant gold, the robes a shining white. At the center was Jesus, his gentle gaze directed outwards, one hand outstretched towards the congregation, the other pointing up to heaven.

Dave couldn't help but think about Aislinn's description of Christ, both his incomprehensible brightness and the intensity of the love of his gaze. This stained-glass Jesus was beautiful but paled in comparison to her description. He wondered what it would be like to feel a love so intense, to be completely accepted and loved just as he was, to be free from guilt and fear. He realized he intensely wanted Aislinn's experience to be true, to have a God who cared that deeply about him and to have a deeper purpose for his life. But so much of her story bordered on the ridiculous. She had struggled to believe in God before her experience. He wondered if perhaps her damaged mind could have contrived an overly vivid dream to satisfy her desires. However, Dave knew that regardless of the truth of her story, the husband he had been these past few weeks was not the one his wife deserved.

He had kept all these emotions bottled up within himself, uncertain of who to turn to or even how to begin to unpack his thoughts. Now, alone in the quiet comfort of the church, he allowed the torrent of emotion to pour out of him, his sobs echoing through the sanctuary. Just acknowledging the pain within himself was healing. His muscles began to relax as his tears slowed. He reached into the pocket of his hoodie and pulled out a tissue of questionable integrity.

"Here—we have extra." A priest was standing at the edge of the wooden pew, holding out a small box of clean tissue. He looked to be in his mid-50's, salt and pepper mixed into his dark brown, almost black hair. Dave immediately recognized the black dress and white clerical collar from the pastors of his childhood and felt calmed by the priest's presence.

"I don't know what brings you here, but I'm certain that He is glad that you came." The priest motioned with his head towards the stained-glass Jesus looking down at them. "May I take a seat?"

"Of course," Dave shifted a few more inches to his right, making room for the older gentleman and accepted the offer of tissues. He considered how to ask the priest about what was weighing on his mind. His eyes rested on the image of Jesus, the image that was a shadow of the true Christ.

"Ever wonder what it would be like to meet him?" Dave asked.

The priest smiled. "Our faith tells us we will one day. I can only imagine what that kind of love would do to a soul. For now, I trust in the words of those who have walked with him on this Earth. That will have to be enough."

Dave nodded. He had hoped for something more. The priest sensed his willingness to talk. "Penny for your thoughts, son?"

Dave exhaled audibly and fumbled with the tissue in his hand. "It's my wife. I feel like I'm already losing her, and we've barely started on our journey together." He glanced over at his silent companion. The clergyman's compassionate, patient expression urged him on.

"We were married a few weeks ago. On our honeymoon, she had an accident out in the ocean and nearly drowned. Ever since, she has been so different from the woman I dated that I feel as though I don't even know her."

"Did she tell you what happened? When she almost died, that is."

Dave looked at the priest with interest. "Well, yes, she did. She said she went to heaven, saw Jesus and talked with him. I'm not sure what to make of it." Dave started talking faster, embarrassed to be admitting to a stranger that he gave credence to a story that, to him, made little logical sense. "She was unconscious for a long time—at least fifteen minutes, and her heart stopped for a good portion of that. But an oxygen-starved brain could create all sorts of hallucinations."

"Does she otherwise seem as though her brain function has suffered?"

Dave shrugged. "No, not at all. In fact, she seems better. She seems healthier and happier. Her co-workers have even told her how much stronger, more creative, and caring of a teacher she is." Dave paused, thinking. "She does have moments when she seems sad, a quiet sadness that she won't talk about with me."

"I would be sad as well if I left heaven." The priest's voice lowered a bit as he ventured to take a guess at what was bothering Dave most. "Your wife is happy and healthy. It sounds to me that what you're struggling with most is making sense of what happened to her."

Dave was grateful for this man's open heart and mind; the priest wasn't judging either Aislinn or him.

"Maybe you're right," Dave admitted. It almost seemed that the priest believed Aislinn's story. "Would you be able to believe her if you were in my place?"

The priest thought for a moment. "Nothing I haven't heard of before. But yes, if I were in your shoes, I would struggle to believe as well."

Dave looked at the older man, surprised. "So, others have had these sorts of experiences before? You think they're real?"

"As real as you and I are right now—perhaps even more so." The priest took a breath. "Over the years I have visited parishioners during their stays in the hospital. I've blessed a few babies, performed some last rites, and visited many recovering from various illnesses and surgeries. You'd be surprised by the number of folks who refused to tell anyone but me their stories, but who experienced something quite akin to what your wife did. Even still, I might not have believed them, but for the chance I've had to be in the room as some of our dear ones have passed over. I've seen them suddenly sit up and look towards the end of bed, talking to relatives they haven't seen for years. And I've felt a few of their spirits pass peacefully next to me, their spiritual forms lingering ever so briefly before me before they go on their way. Your wife's story, it's true."

The priest sat quietly beside Dave and let the import of his words sink in. Even an empty church was never silent and the slight creaking of the wood settling in the large building was somehow comforting. Dave relaxed as he more fully accepted the truth of Aislinn's story. As he thought more, he realized that it was the only sensible conclusion. First there were the seven-foot-tall men who mysteriously disappeared, followed by Aislinn's miraculous recovery. Then there was Aislinn's heightened intelligence and intuition—something a creation of her oxygen-starved brain could not explain. Finally, she seemed whole and present. As he worked through the evidence from this logical perspective, Dave realized only one conclusion made sense. Aislinn really had experienced heaven. And if her experience wasn't a figment of her imagination, if it were true, then the intense love of Christ and God's acceptance of our flaws, the deep purpose of our lives...it was all true as well. The enormity of this realization struck him suddenly.

"It's all real. All of it." He paused. "And she left that beauty in part to be with me." Something inside him broke as he realized both the intensity of her love for him and how much she might be now regretting her decision to return, the fool that he had been recently.

A fresh tear made its way down his cheek. He hoped that he could still be the man that she left heaven to return to.

There was one nagging doubt that had plagued Dave these last several weeks. "Before the incident, I was her calm when she was anxious, her hope when she was afraid. Now, she is the calm one. Does she even need me anymore?"

The priest laid his hand on Dave's shoulder. "More so than ever, just differently. When you look at her, knowing the truth of who she is and who you are, you bring back the love of heaven that she so dearly misses. You are her connection to her spiritual home."

Dave felt the compassion of the priest. In that moment, he was the hands and heart of Christ to him. Dave doubted his ability to be the same to Aislinn. Being the love of heaven to her was far from the man Dave had been those past few weeks. As for living the truth of who they really were, he wasn't sure he yet knew the truth, let alone how to live it. "I, I don't know how to do that," he stuttered.

"God will help you," the priest said. "There is nothing he wants more than for you to learn your identity in Christ and to live that truth. If you ask for his help, he will not fail you." He stood up and reached out his hand to Dave, offering a firm handshake. "God go with you."

Dave sat listening to the priest's footsteps, the echo gradually receding. The sun had nearly set, and the candlelight alone lit the alter. Dave thought of one of the Bible stories he had read as a child, about a man who brought his sick son to Jesus and exclaimed, "Lord, I believe; help my unbelief."[124] Dave bowed his head. For the first time in many years, he had genuine faith in something higher than himself.

Quietly, in a whisper, he prayed. "Jesus, I believe that what Aislinn experienced is real. I believe that you are real and that you see me and love me as I am. Please help me to be the husband that Aislinn deserves. Help me to bring the wife you've given me a little bit of the heaven she left behind."

Suddenly, Dave felt the stress, fear, and guilt of the past month fall away from him, as if strong spiritual hands were opening his chest and removing all the baggage that he carried within him. In its place, an overpowering wave of peace and love filled him. He felt as if his body were floating a few inches off the pew. Gradually, the feeling began to fade, and the tightness crept back. Then, as if he had asked for an encore, everything happened again; this time, the waves of love were stronger. As the second wave slowly faded, Dave opened his eyes. They were wet with tears.[125]

"Nothing is impossible with God," he whispered, choked up. Dave imagined it would take years if not lifetimes of spiritual transformation to regularly carry within him the power of the love he felt in the empty church that evening. But he knew now that he would not be making the journey alone.

18

Miracles

As time passed, Dave and Aislinn were in the process of becoming something entirely new. Aislinn's experience had opened Dave's heart to the truth and day by day they both were becoming a reflection of the love of heaven. Dave became more at ease with Aislinn's uncanny ability to read his mind, and came to love her new, easy peace. They could spend an hour or more simply watching a sunset or basking in the glow of a fire, hand-in-hand, silently enjoying each other's company.

Besides Aislinn's new calm, there were other small changes that required a bit of adjustment. She quickly learned that she couldn't wear a watch—electronics frequently malfunctioned when she was in close proximity. This mystified both her and Dave, but they slowly learned to work around the inconvenience. She drove the older of their two cars, which had fewer electronic components, and no longer carried her cell phone right next to her body. Her school computer had held so far, but she minimized her use of it, just in case.

She would also occasionally have hunches about future events—weather events and happenings in their extended family and close friends—and had yet to be wrong. This was helpful when they dodged getting stuck driving in a severe thunderstorm, but awkward when they had to feign surprise over Aislinn cousin's pregnancy.[126]

As they settled into their new married life, Aislinn surprised Dave with a border collie puppy. She knew the new puppy wouldn't replace Zeus' place in Dave's heart. However, Dave loved having a dog around and she hoped it would be a joyful addition to their lives—the puppy might even get Toby up off the couch now and again.

"This cutie might replace some of the spunk that you miss in me," Aislinn joked.

Dave laughed. His face was being covered in slobbery kisses. He tried to keep the energetic little one calm long enough to respond.

"I love you just as much if not more now than I did before, sweetheart. But this little girl is a wonderful addition to our family."

"She'll need a name," Aislinn said.

"That's easy," Dave replied. "She looks like a Hera to me. Plus, I have the feeling that with us two pushovers, she'll be in charge around here."

A few days later, Dave and Hera had just come in from a game of frisbee at the park. It was a colder night and Dave was chilled. Hera, having done the bulk of the exercise, was worn out and happily curled up in the corner with her favorite chew toy, a simple rawhide wishbone. Dave was excited to spend the evening watching a movie with his wife in front of a warm fire. Thus far, Hera and Toby were getting along quite well now and might even end up on either side of them—a true family affair.

"Do we have any more old newspaper? The downdraft is really making things difficult tonight." Dave poked at the pitiful smoking mass—the only result his efforts had produced thus far.

"Yeah. No problem." Aislinn hopped up and grabbed yesterday's paper from the recycling bin. Suddenly, Dave's grandmother's face flashed across her consciousness. The scenery around her faded and for what could only have lasted for a fraction of a second, Aislinn saw the older woman before her and felt her physical and emotional pain. The visual was as vivid as her experiences in heaven—she saw with her soul, not her mind. Aislinn knew instantly that something was wrong.

"Dave—It's Grandmom—we need to go to her—now." Dave's grandmother, Grace, lived about five miles north of their apartment. At the age of 83, she still lived alone and was in good health.

"What's going on?"

"I saw her—she was bent over in pain, mentally calling for help. I don't know if it's a heart attack, stroke, or something else, but she needs immediate medical assistance."

Dave didn't hesitate. He tossed a glass of water on the sparks and abruptly closed off the fireplace, coughing at the resulting smoke. "Call 911. I'll start the car."

The ambulance reached Grace's condo a few minutes before Dave and Aislinn. By the time they arrived, the EMT's were carrying Grace out on a stretcher.

Dave looked at Aislinn wide-eyed, still flummoxed by her new abilities and scared for his grandmother's life.

Aislinn took Dave's hands into hers and looked calmly into his eyes.

"She'll be okay. I promise."

Dave nodded and inhaled sharply, shaking a bit. Aislinn wrapped her arms around him, the two of them clinging to each other for comfort as the sound of the sirens faded.

About forty-five minutes later, they arrived at the emergency department and were ushered to Grace's room, being quickly identified as family.

Dave knocked gently on the door. Grace was propped up on pillows, looking tired but alert.

"Dave…Aislinn…" she greeted them, a small smile turning up the corners of her lips. "The EMTs told me the call came from your number. I was just sitting there on the couch, watching the news, when I felt tightness in my arm and had trouble catching my breath. Before I realized what was going on, they were pounding on my door. I don't know how you knew, but I'm grateful."

Dave squeezed Aislinn's hand.

"It's a miracle," Grace continued. "If you hadn't made that call, I might not be here." She leaned back, her usually neatly styled snow-white curls flattened by the pressure of the pillow on the back of her head. She looked from Dave to Aislinn and smiled. Aislinn blushed, unsure of what to tell Grace.

"What did the doctor say, Grandmom?" Dave said, concerned about Grace's welfare and hoping to save Aislinn an awkward and long explanation. He had easily figured out from the little she had shared that his grandmother had suffered a heart attack.

"The nurses have me hooked up to this bag of goodies," she gestured at her IV pole, "And the doctor says they're supposed to prevent any further damage to my ticker. I certainly am feeling better, so that's a good sign."

"I guess they'll be running you through a bunch of tests in a bit," Aislinn said.

"Oh, I'm sure of it. But there's no need to worry. After what happened so far today, I'm quite sure that it is not my time to leave this world just yet." She turned to look at Dave, and put her free hand on top of his, looking up at him lovingly. Aislinn sensed Dave might want to be alone with her for a little bit, and she excused herself to get a drink.

The sound of Grace's voice gradually faded as Aislinn wound her way through the halls of the ER in search of a refreshing cup of coffee and a chance to process all that had just transpired. She wondered at the cause of these visions and premonitions. She considered that they might be the result of her realization of her interconnectedness with all that surrounded her. However, Aislinn did not rule out the possibility that she had "suffered" some sort of brain trauma that made these communications and experiences possible. At the very least, her beliefs in what was possible within their human forms had expanded.

She spotted a sign indicating the direction of the main lobby and made a sharp right turn, mentally making a note of her path so that she could later retrace her steps back to Dave and Grace. Aislinn was passing the last few rooms in the ER when she heard sobbing within one to her left. Emotionally sensitive from the events of the day, she paused and leaned towards the entryway. The tears were coming from a small boy—maybe seven or eight years old. His coarse brown hair formed a messy mop on his head, covering his ears and falling within an inch of his eyes. His small fists rubbed his eyes as he struggled to pull himself together. A woman lay in the bed, attached to several monitors and IV medications. She looked young, most likely the boy's mother. Another woman was gently comforting the boy, bending down close to him, speaking softly. Aislinn stepped away from view, her back flat against the wall. She felt a tightness in her chest and her eyes watered. It was an involuntary reaction, this connectedness to the boy, her soul uniting with his and experiencing his inner agony. She took a few deep breaths, closed her eyes, and centered herself on what was now her constant truth—the deep peace of knowing that all was well and in harmony, all connected in the divine essence of God. Aislinn sent love to the boy and his ailing mother. She must have stood there for minutes in prayer, doing the only thing that seemed right under the circumstances, participating in silent communion with these hurting souls.

A few months prior, prayer for this family would have been a desperate, fearful pleading. Now Aislinn felt a deep acceptance of whatever would come—God would ensure that all things happened according to his will. All would be well. There was a heavy peace to her prayer mixed with the hope that the best of what could be would bless this family.

In her mind's eye, she was the eight-year-old boy, scanning the bleachers at his little league game for his mom, seeing her cheering him on, his heart overflowing with gratitude to still have her with him, healthy and vibrant. He was folded in his mother's warm embrace, her blonde hair tickling his cheek and her hand ruffling his hair. He was going on vacation with her, enjoying looking for seashells and chasing seagulls. Aislinn felt the deep connectedness with this boy that was the nature of existence in her spirit form—it permeated her being again.

She took a deep breath and sent one last surge of positive healing energy to the woman, feeling a current of warmth rush through her body as she did so.[127] Then, bringing herself back to her surroundings, she took a deep breath and refocused her attention on her briefly abandoned coffee run.

Grace remained in the hospital for two days as the medical professionals got to the core of her heart ailment and set her on a path of preventative meds and lifestyle changes. No permanent damage had been sustained and Grace was released with an order to walk regularly and take a blood thinner once daily.

"At 83, I just appreciate that they still give a darn about whether I tack on a few more years to my life." Grace held tightly to Dave's arm as Dave helped her out of the car and back to her home. "I suppose I'll give the meds and exercise a go—maybe I'll live long enough to see a great-granddaughter." She winked at Aislinn.

"If we are so blessed, Grandmom," Aislinn said. "Or a great-grandson, of course."

"Pshh, it'll be a girl—Dave needs a daughter to reel him in."

Dave laughed and shrugged, indifferent to the gender of any future children.

"Speaking of daughters, well I'll be darned if a miracle didn't happen in the ER the night I was admitted."

Dave and Aislinn shifted their focus quickly to Grace, their hearts and minds attuned to such stories after their honeymoon experience.

"My nurse told me a 30-year-old single mom was admitted an hour or so before me that first night—terminal cancer patient, who by all appearances was taking a turn for the worse. By midnight, she seemed to have revived a bit. And wouldn't you know, the next day, her scans came back and showed the cancer was receding! Nurse had never seen anything like it. And a good thing too, what with a young boy to care for."

Aislinn's heart filled with gratitude for the healing; the boy would have his mother by his side for quite a while longer.

"I suppose that actually makes two miracles in one night," Grace continued. "Not sure how anyone can doubt the goodness of God after a night like that."

19

This Side of the Jordan

The evening after Grace's release, after a quiet dinner, both of them consumed in their thoughts, Aislinn retreated to the small field behind their home to meditate and pray. Large mounds of ankle-high light brown grass, dormant for the winter season, provided a natural resting spot beside a meandering stream that split the field in two. Her perch was a few feet above the stream which had, over the decades, formed a gully. Large rocks created small obstructions to the water's flow, creating calming ripples in the stream's path. The soothing trickling sound of the gentle waterfall pulled her into a trance-like state. Aislinn's mind wandered to the walks with Jesus just a few months before and the lessons that were relayed to her while she was in her spirit-form. Those lessons had eliminated her fear of death and given new meaning to her Earthly years to come. Each breath was a new opportunity for loving service to what Aislinn now understood was an extension of her own essence.

She looked over her shoulder. Dave had been silently watching her from the patio, two glasses of wine in his hands. Aislinn smiled, welcoming his interruption to her silent reflections. He made his way across the field, his feet clumsily making their way over the grass mounds, a few drops of wine spilling over the sides of the glasses. Hera bounded after him, her small body disappearing behind the larger mounds. Dave settled in next to Aislinn and handed her one of the glasses of cabernet.

"Here's to Grandmom's coming home, and to you, Aislinn."

"To Grandmom, and to miracles." She touched her glass to his, the ring reverberating through the long stem of the glass. They both took a sip and returned their gaze to the stream.

"You had something to do with that single mother's healing too, didn't you?" Dave's question broke the calming meditative sound of the gently flowing water.

Aislinn carefully crafted her response, unsure of how much she should reveal of her intuitive sense of how things played out. "I prayed for her; more than that, I can't know for sure."

Dave nodded. The sun began to slip below the horizon, painting the sky with a palette of vivid colors.

"Thank you, Aislinn," Dave finally said.

"It was God, not me."

"No, not Grandmom's healing, although, believe me, I'm grateful for that as well." Dave paused. He looked at her, his eyes dancing, and he squeezed her hand tighter. "Thank you for the gift of faith. I thought I was living before. But now—it's like I'm starting over, and this time, everything has greater depth and meaning. You gave me a new life, Aislinn."

Aislinn looked into his eyes. Dave, too, had changed. Though he had always been a kind, loving man, he now moved and lived with greater purpose. He still had his fun-loving nature, but there was a gravity to him that was new to her. He seemed steadier and more at peace, even more the rock in her life than he had been before.

Hera bounded through the stream in front of them, lapping at the water and then scampered up the bank to explore the other shore. Dave laughed. The puppy's energy seemed limitless.

The water calmed behind Hera and resumed its course, easily forging a path around the obstacles in its way.

Like the stream, Aislinn knew they would meet with obstacles and challenges in the years to come. That was the reason they were on Earth to begin with. However, their deep peace and trust in the flow of life would guide them through. There would be days when one or both of them would again briefly lose themselves in the intensity of the trials sure to come. But they would be just that, days. They would learn from those challenges and their souls would grow in maturity and strength. The peace and deep rootedness they now had could never be taken from them.

"If only everyone could have this deep assurance," she said.

The sun continued to drop below the horizon, waves of color splayed out across the sky, the light reflected by the water below. "Someday," Dave said. "Until that someday comes, we will do our part to bring heaven to Earth."

Dave took Aislinn's hand in his. It was one of the most beautiful sunsets they had ever seen, as if a reflection of the immense gratitude they felt within. The kingdom of heaven was alive and well in their hearts and the future lay ahead, filled with possibility.

Reading Group Guide

Chapters 1 & 2

1. Aislinn feels more anchored in the presence of her grandfather. His slow, mindful pace of living is inspiring to her, and his deep faith gives her hope in one day regaining her own faith in God. Who in your life is a role model? What can you learn from their example?
2. Do you relate to Aislinn's difficulty with keeping her attention focused on the present moment? Why or why not?
3. Aislinn struggles immensely with her faith after losing Allie. She struggles to reconcile a loving God with the pain she experienced and with the suffering she sees in the world. When have you struggled with your faith?
4. What is the relationship between faith and character? Is it possible to be a good person without faith? Is it possible to have genuine faith and yet still live an immoral life?
5. Dave tells Aislinn that being angry with God is still a form of belief. What are your thoughts? Have you ever experienced this?

Chapters 3 & 4

1. How does Aislinn's experience of death compare to your own expectations prior to reading this work? What did you find surprising from Aislinn's experience, if anything?
2. Aislinn feels a sense of being simultaneously both a unique individual and united with everything. This reminds her of the nature of the Trinity. How might Aislinn's experience enhance your understanding of the Holy Trinity?
3. When Aislinn arrives on the spiritual plane, her environment is created from her memories to be a calming, welcoming place. Where do you feel most "at home"? What environment do you find most calming and why?
4. Pop explains that heaven is all there is and that dying is more a waking up to reality than a change in location. What are your thoughts?

5. How is suffering part of the growing process? How have you grown from the pain in your life? Do you think such growth would have been possible without your painful experience? Why or why not?
6. Aislinn is not judged in her life review, though she is held responsible for her actions. Some faith traditions teach that God judges and punishes sin, others that faith covers sin and the slate is wiped clean. What do you believe?
7. Aislinn learns that it is the state of her heart or her motives, not the actions themselves, that matter. Looking back on your own life, when did the state of your heart not align with your actions, either for good or ill?
8. Read Psalm 139: 1 – 18. Considering these verses as well as Aislinn's experience at the end of Chapter 4, how should we view ourselves and why?

Chapters 5 & 6

1. Read 1 Corinthians 12:12-27. How do these verses relate to Aislinn's experience of the heavenly city?
2. When have you viewed the growth and experiences of another as being as important as your own? What was the result?
3. Read Revelation 21:9-22:5. What similarities do you notice between the city in Revelation and the one Aislinn sees? What are the differences?
4. When have you struggled to enjoy the journey? Does any of Pop's advice seem beneficial for keeping a proper perspective?
5. Aislinn realizes that she is eternally connected to those she loves. When have you felt a connection to someone, whether living or dead, when they were not physically present?
6. Much of chapter 6 touches on topics that are not included in the typical Christian canon, such as life on other planets and reincarnation. These topics are included as they are the consensus from most individuals who have had an NDE. What are your thoughts on these topics? Does reading this work at all change your opinions? Regardless, do you think

your opinion on these topics meaningfully affects your life choices or is it more important to focus on the here and now?
7. What difference would it make if you were confident that there was a plan for your life, a plan that you agreed to before your birth and that you knew was in your best interest? Would this bring comfort during the uncertainties and trials?

Chapters 7 & 8

1. Aislinn admits that there were many times when she felt the presence of the spiritual plane while in her Earthly body. What experiences have you had that may have been nudges from an angel or guide or a gentle redirection on your life's path?
2. Consider what Jesus tells Aislinn about the value of separation from the spiritual plane. Do you believe an illusion of separation from the divine is helpful for the soul's growth? Why or why not?
3. When, like Chris, have you obeyed the Holy Spirit's/angel's/guide's direction? What was the result?
4. What did you grow up believing about hell? Did it align with your understanding of God's character? Did this story challenge or change your thinking in any way?
5. Bob's choices led him further and further from God. When have you found yourself going down a similar slippery slope? What pulled you back?
6. Bob almost falls for the half-truth of the demons, that the path back to God is more horrifying and difficult than the road he is already on. What half-truths have you been tempted to believe on your faith journey?
7. The demons cannot bear to be in the presence of God. Yet God would welcome them with open arms if ever they turned, open-hearted, willing to be healed. Read and pray Psalm 86, confident in God's ever-present love for you.

Chapters 9-11

1. Chapter 9 may pose challenges for some. How did you react to this perspective on Jesus being the way, the truth, and the life? How does this align with your concept of the nature of God? What issues come up for you as you consider the NDE perspective?
2. In the story, Jesus tells Aislinn that people would draw closer to the truth by sharing and building on each other's beliefs than by attacking and breaking each other down for their faith. What are your thoughts? When have you learned and benefited from another faith tradition?
3. As they near the core, Jesus and Aislinn commune with souls whose joy is so overwhelming that they cannot help but sing. When have you experienced this sort of joy in your life? What state of mind or heart made this experience possible for you?
4. The highest level of heaven was the point of creation itself—where new matter was coming into being. We are made in the image of God and thus we too have a strong desire to create. Not all of us have traditional artistic or musical talent, yet creating something new, whether a concept, equation, game, or joke, is still a form of creativity. When and how do you create? What draws you to create? How does the process of creating fulfill you?
5. Consider the scene of the boy on the mountainside. When has God helped you through a difficult scenario? When were you left to figure something out "on your own"? What was the result?
6. How has the practice of prayer transformed you? Which type of prayer, gratitude or petition, do you gravitate towards? Why?
7. Jesus takes Aislinn to the mountainside to witness a thunderstorm. When have you seen the wisdom of nature in action?
8. What is the mind's role in our physical bodies on Earth? How does your understanding of how the mind works and Jesus' warning to heed spiritual guidance give new meaning

to Jesus' words in the Bible, "The spirit is willing, but the flesh is weak"?

Chapter 12

1. Jesus recommends frequently practicing a more contemplative form of prayer. Have you ever spent extended time listening? If not, what would it take to set a regular time aside each day to simply tune into the voice of the Spirit, as Jesus did?
2. Read Luke 10:38-42. What is the "one thing that matters" that Jesus speaks of? Why do you think it so difficult to stay focused on what Jesus so clearly says is a priority?
3. What one command of Jesus' are you focusing on right now? How does it relate back to the greatest commandment (love God, love self, love others)?
4. What other spiritual teachers have you found especially helpful? These teachers can be people you know or spiritual masters whose works you have studied. What important lessons did they teach you?
5. Jesus emphasizes the power of human thought to transform the reality of our lives. When have you noticed your thoughts affecting your reality and the well-being of those close to you? What steps can you take to transform your thoughts and emotions so that they reflect God's truth and his heart?

Chapters 13 - 14

1. What do you think of Jesus' plan in the story (love the person in front of you)? When have you seen love transform others?
2. What is the difference between loving and being love? What is your experience with each?
3. When have you reacted negatively to someone and later realized that the behavior that bothered you was also within yourself? Take time to consider if there are other

relationships or gripes you have with others that may point to areas for self-reflection and growth.
4. What teachers and messengers has God put into your life? What lessons have you learned from them? What lessons do you think God is currently teaching you through these relationships?
5. In many places in the Hebrew Scriptures/Old Testament, God levels consequences on groups of people, from the plagues in Egypt to the Babylonian Exile. In Chapter 13, Jesus says that wars and other disasters often happen because, as a collective, we desire a certain outcome or need to learn a certain lesson. What are your thoughts on this?
6. Read Isaiah 65: 17-25. Compare and contrast Isaiah's prophecy with the idyllic Earth described in chapter 13. What are your thoughts about/reactions to this potential future?

Chapters 15 – 19

1. What changes do you notice in Aislinn after her experience? Consider especially her outlook on life and interactions with others.
2. Aislinn gets a glimpse of "heaven" when watching the volleyball game on the beach. What situations have you encountered where the sense of oneness and compassion for others, typical for the spiritual plane, prevail?
3. Dave struggles with the new Aislinn. However, as the priest points out, it is not Aislinn herself that he is troubled by. Instead, he is wrestling with how to relate to Aislinn and to God, in light of her supposed NDE. Becoming honest with himself is the first step to his healing. Where in your life do you need to be honest with yourself and with others about what you are struggling with?
4. The priest urges Dave to be the love of heaven to Aislinn by reflecting the truth of who she is back to her. How can you offer this gift to those in your life?
5. What is unique about how Aislinn prays for the mother and son at the hospital? How might this example change how you approach praying for others?

6. Dave thanks Aislinn for the depth and meaning that her experience has added to his life. How has Aislinn's story impacted you? How is your life different now that you know what waits for you on the other side of the Jordan?

Acknowledgements

I wish to acknowledge, first and foremost, my family. My husband, Brett Chrest, who walked alongside me on our writing journeys, publishing his own book in 2021, days before his passing. I bounced ideas off him from the beginning, years ago. His suggestions, criticisms, and stylistic help were instrumental to the success of this work. Thank you, Brett, for your endless patience, creativity, and most of all, for your unconditional love. I am grateful to have been on this journey of life with you and feel strongly the thread forever connecting us.

Our sons, Brooks and Brandon, for their patience with Mama's incessant talk of the spiritual and especially with both Mama and Daddy during this final summer before publication. You mean the world to us, and we are forever proud of you.

My wonderful friends and critics, Mary Beth Naish, Alice Bonthron, Mark Boschert, Linda Boschert, and Terri Wytko. Their feedback, especially on the early drafts, gave life to the story.

All those who have had an NDE and whose works and stories have contributed in some way to this book, especially Nancy Rynes, who gave an NDEer's personal perspective on the final draft.

Finally, I am forever grateful to God as well as to those who have passed over before us who have been there to guide us. Thank you for inspiring this small miracle of a work into being.

About the Author

Leah Chrest serves as a high-school math teacher. She has had a lifelong passion for all things spiritual and enjoys practicing and teaching mindfulness and meditation. She lives in Maryland with her two children. Visit her at www.thecontemplativechristian.com and at her YouTube channel at www.youtube.com/c/christianmeditation.

Notes

[1] A detailed description of death by drowning in rapids comes from both Sandra's and Jennifer's NDEs.
Sandra H NDE 3578. (n.d.) *NDERF*. Retrieved from https://www.nderf.org/Experiences/1sandra_h_nde.html
Jennifer W NDE 7516. (n.d.) *NDERF*. Retrieved from https://www.nderf.org/Experiences/1jennifer_w_nde_7516.html

[2] Most of the NDEs I encountered, regardless of the means of death, agreed that the process of dying is not as painful as a person would expect watching the scene from an outsider's perspective. Once death is accepted, the soul leaves the body behind. The body still reacts—screaming, writhing, visibly in pain, depending on the cause of death, but the soul experiences none of this once the death is accepted. Mary Neal speaks about this in detail in her recounting of her experience and suggests this should give us comfort when we see or know of loved ones struggling prior to death.
Mary C Neal, M.D. (2017). *7 Lessons from Heaven: How Dying Taught Me to Live a Joy-Filled Life*. Convergent Books.

[3] A few NDEs mentioned a popping/plopping sound as the soul disconnected from the body. Beatrice shares about the feeling of leaving the body and the "plopping" sound.
Beatrice W NDE 9251. (n.d.) *NDERF*. Retrieved from https://www.nderf.org/Experiences/1beatrice_w_nde.html

[4] 1 Thessalonians 4:14-15

[5] Many NDEs refer to an immediate disassociation from the body. Often, immediately following death, the spirit sees the body's form and feels no attachment to it--no more than a person would a piece of furniture. This shows the stark divide between life in the body (the struggle to stay alive) that precedes the transition and life apart from the body (where the body is disregarded). Niels details his indifference towards his body in his NDE.
Niels W NDE 9193. (n.d.) *NDERF*. Retrieved from https://www.nderf.org/Experiences/1niels_w_nde.html

[6] Some NDEs describe a peaceful darkness (like Roger), others being surrounded by brilliant light (like Juliet), and others a combination of both. Perhaps the environment is somehow both dark and light and each experiencer interprets it differently. Alternately, each NDE may be different due to the needs of the soul (whatever scene would be most comforting is what is encountered). In all cases, there is a deep sense of peace and oneness with everything.

Juliet N NDE 10077 (n.d.) *NDERF*. Retrieved from:
https://www.nderf.org/Experiences/1juliet_n_nde.html
Roger C NDE 744 (n.d.) *NDERF*. Retrieved from:
https://www.nderf.org/Experiences/1roger_c_nde.html

[7] Anelia's NDE is just one example of what is found in the vast majority of NDEs—a sense that the way time passes on the "other side" cannot be put into words.

Anelia G NDE 9108 (n.d.) *NDERF*. Retrieved from:
https://www.nderf.org/Experiences/1anelia_g_nde.html

[8] The transition from earthly to heavenly consciousness is again, a stark divide. Consciousness expands upon death. When a physical landscape is encountered, it is far more intense than the Earthly plane. Colors are more varied and vibrant, the experience of all senses more intense. Barbara's description of the vivid environment in her NDE experience is typical of many.

Barbara D. NDE 8419 (n.d.) *NDERF*. Retrieved from
https://www.nderf.org/Experiences/1barbara_d_nde.html

[9] Nancy explains that the environment shifted in its energy based on her emotions.

Rynes, Nancy (2015). *Awakenings from the Light: 12 Life Lessons from a Near-Death Experience*. [Kindle Cloud Reader Version]. Retrieved from amazon.com.

[10] Another interesting feature is the intermingling of the senses—colors can be felt, and plants tasted without touching them. Bizarrely, at least 2 accounts (including Bill's) suggest that the grass "tastes" like watermelon.

Bill W. NDE 180 (n.d.) *NDERF*. Retrieved from
https://www.nderf.org/Experiences/1bill_w_nde.html

[11] 360-degree vision is common in many experiences. Leonard's is a nice example.

Leonard NDE 4046 (n.d.) *NDERF*. Retrieved from
https://www.nderf.org/Experiences/1leonard_nde.html

[12] Knowledge transmission is intuitive. Experiencers discuss a sense of simply "knowing" certain things are true. Unlike on Earth, when we may doubt our intuitive feelings, this knowing is definite. Gary's initial NDE experience is without a "Guide," just like Aislinn's, and he describes his intuitive understanding.

Gary D NDE 2428 (n.d.) *NDERF*. Retrieved from
https://www.nderf.org/Experiences/1gary_d_nde.html

[13] Several NDEs, John's included, mention seeing a heavenly city in the distance.

John F. NDE 61 (n.d.). *NDERF*. Retrieved from
https://www.nderf.org/Experiences/1john_f_nde.html

[14] Although for ease of narration, I describe her as "walking" through most of the book, movement on the other side appears to occur more through thought and is more of a drifting from one location to another. Gary describes this movement based on desire and focus-based movement well.
   Gary D. NDE 2428 (n.d.) *NDERF.* Retrieved from https://www.nderf.org/Experiences/1gary_d_nde.html

[15] In many cases, loved ones appear vibrant and healthy and are young in appearance. Penny recounts meeting her young-looking great-grandmother. Interestingly, some experiencers, like Sharon, also meet souls who died as fetuses, infants, or children—these beings also appear as healthy young adults.
   Penny C. NDE 7234 (n.d.) *NDERF.* Retrieved from https://www.nderf.org/Experiences/1penny_c_nde.html
   Sharon M. NDE 7925 (n.d.) *NDERF.* Retrieved from https://www.nderf.org/Experiences/1sharon_m_nde_7925.html

[16] Communication with beings is telepathic. Everything—thoughts, emotions, even the essence of the soul itself is clearly communicated without words. Deception appears to be impossible. Bobbi goes into beautiful detail about this aspect of her experience, and it is well worth the read.
   Bobbi D NDE 4022 (n.d.) *NDERF.* Retrieved from https://www.nderf.org/Experiences/1bobbi_d_nde.html

[17] In Rev. Storm's NDE, he is informed that each soul is escorted home differently, depending on the particulars of their life, their culture, and the extent of their spiritual understanding. He is told that the reason for this is that God values each soul's uniqueness. This revelation to Storm matches what can be seen throughout other NDEs—through some common elements are present in all NDEs (heightened consciousness, overwhelming feeling of love and peace, etc.), each initial experience is different. Some souls are greeted by angelic beings, some by relatives, and others no one at all. The "landscape" can vary greatly, as can the events of the NDE. We are each given what we need most to help in the transition when our souls move on.
   Storm, Howard. (2005). *My Descent into Death: A Second Chance at Life.* Doubleday. P 51-52

[18] Regardless of the type of death, those who experience an NDE make clear that the soul leaves the body long before the physical death of the body. In an e-mail conversation I had with Nancy Rynes, whose book I cite frequently in this work, she explains: "In heart attack victims, their soul often leaves before they even register what's going on or have feelings of pain. In patients dying from long term illness, their soul can leave hours to

days before the body dies (but as or just after they go into the final coma). There are angelic types of beings that are kind of on standby to assist, but in general, the transition out of the body is gentle and requires no conscious thought on the soul's part. Most will hear the Music of Heaven and feel the Love, but the whole thing just unfolds easily, kind of like waking up from sleep in the morning."

[19] Throughout NDEs, transitions between scenes are instantaneous and free of stress. Roger shifts from planet to planet in a seamless fashion in his NDE.

Roger C NDE 744 (n.d.) *NDERF.* Retrieved from:
https://www.nderf.org/Experiences/1roger_c_nde.html

[20] Nancy explains that the environment shifted in its energy based on her emotions.

Rynes, Nancy (2015). *Awakenings from the Light: 12 Life Lessons from a Near-Death Experience.* [Kindle Cloud Reader Version]. Retrieved from amazon.com.

[21] Sylvia learns that her weak physical form and her draw to nursing were all challenges to help her to grow.

Sylvia W NDE 152 (n.d.) *NDERF.* Retrieved from:
https://www.nderf.org/Experiences/1sylvia_w_nde.html

[22] Rev Storm explains the general set-up of his life review clearly, explaining how the important aspects of each scene are emphasized.

Storm, Howard. (2005). *My Descent into Death: A Second Chance at Life.* Doubleday. P 30-31

[23] Glauco explains how he can feel the pain he caused others, but also notes the absence of judgment from his guide.

Glauco S NDE 3674 (n.d.) *NDERF.* Retrieved from:
https://www.nderf.org/Experiences/1glauco_s_nde.html

[24] In almost all NDE life reviews (a very common part of NDEs), the only judgment is from the self. Even that judgment seems to be less intense than it would be on Earth. I appreciated Juliet's take that the "ego" is removed from the situation and thus we experience only conviction and the desirability of a different course, rather than paralyzing guilt. Most experiencers note that their guides do not judge them but are there in a supportive role.

Juliet N NDE 10077 (n.d.) *NDERF.* Retrieved from:
https://www.nderf.org/Experiences/1juliet_n_nde.html

[25] Rev. Storm emphasizes how his life review highlighted the effects of his actions, including healthy and unhealthy expressions of love, compassion, and those that were out of self-interest vs. the interest of others. The point of the life review was to grow and to learn.

Storm, Howard. (2005). *My Descent into Death: A Second Chance at Life.*

Doubleday. P 30-37.

Hafur highlights the importance of consciously choosing love and learning to choose love, not pain or suffering, in each situation. The life review assists in teaching these lessons to the soul.

Hafur NDE 3558 (n.d.) *NDERF*. Retrieved from https://www.nderf.org/Experiences/1hafur_nde.html

[26] Leonard comments that his life review was emotionally painful, even though there was no judgment involved. He felt the pain he caused others by his choices and proposes that someone who made decisions that injured many (Leonard names Hitler) must have had an agonizing life review.

Leonard NDE 4046 (n.d.) *NDERF*. Retrieved from https://www.nderf.org/Experiences/1leonard_nde.html

[27] Some of the actions that were seen as valuable by the guides or that elicited a positive response from the viewer were of a surprising nature. Mohammad's re-experience of watering a tree in his life review was heartwarming and I wanted the capture the essence of that moment in Aislinn's as well.

Mohammad Z NDE 16083 (n.d.) *NDERF*. Retrieved from: https://www.nderf.org/Experiences/1mohammad_z_nde.html

[28] 1 Samuel 16:7

[29] Though this theme is present in NDE stories, this particular dialogue is reminiscent of one I had with my grandfather towards the end of his life. As I learned from my father, aunts, and uncles, he spoke truth—the man he was at 90 bore little resemblance in spiritual maturity to his younger self. Jean's NDE highlights this truth as well. In her first NDE as a child, Jean is told by a light being/"the Light" about something in her future that she believed she could never do. The light explains that she will mature spiritually throughout her life until she is capable.

Jean NDE 32 (n.d.) *NDERF*. Retrieved from http://dream-prophecy.blogspot.com/2014/07/life-is-ripple-effect-near-death.html

[30] Anita shares that one of the most important lessons she learned in her NDE is how loved we all are. She shares that the more we realize how much we are loved and extend that love inwards to ourselves, the more we are able to recognize the beauty of the world and others.

Anita M NDE 2766/11068 (n.d.) *NDERF*. Retrieved from https://www.nderf.org/Experiences/1anita_m_nde.html

[31] This experience comes straight from Crystal's NDE. This is one of my favorite moments from any experience I have read over the past few years.

McVea, Crystal and Tresniowski, Alex. (2013). *Waking Up in Heaven: A True Story of Brokenness, Heaven, and Life Again*. Howard Books.

[32] Sheila's NDE contains a very beautiful and lengthy conversation with Jesus. When she first meets Jesus, she is overcome by the feeling of his love (specifically for her) that emanated from him. Once she acclimates to the feeling of love in his presence, she "stands" and spends time with him. She feels powerful and glorious in his presence, as well as adored. Sheila says that she realized "We are so powerful and magnificent, and we don't see it in ourselves."
Shelia S NDE 9025 (n.d.) *NDERF*. Retrieved from https://www.nderf.org/Experiences/1sheila_s_nde.html

[33] Nancy's guide emphasizes the importance of self-compassion. We are each amazing and unique and ought to celebrate that uniqueness and fully realize just how beautifully we are created by God.
Rynes, Nancy (2015). *Awakenings from the Light: 12 Life Lessons from a Near-Death Experience*. [Kindle Cloud Reader Version]. Retrieved from amazon.com. Location No. 863, 1136-1179

[34] George Ritchie experiences the brilliant light of the heavenly city from far off. Experiencing a bright, loving, wise light is a very common experience in many NDEs, whether or not a city is seen. See Melinda's for one example.
Williams, Kevin (Sept 26, 2019) "George Ritchie's Near-Death Experience" *Near-Death Experiences and the Afterlife*. Retrieved from https://near-death.com/george-ritchie-nde/
Melinda G NDE 9029 (n.d.) *NDERF*. Retrieved from https://www.nderf.org/Experiences/1melinda_g_nde.html

[35] One of the most NDE elements is reaching a barrier which the soul cannot pass—that point of no return. For Brandy, this is a very high fence, but a wide range of "barriers" appear in NDEs. Once again, each NDE is specialized for the individual's needs.
Brandelyn W NDE 2238 (n.d.) *NDERF*. Retrieved from https://www.nderf.org/Experiences/1brandelyn_w_nde.html

[36] Randy sees brilliant European castle-like buildings in the city with multi-colored domes and multi-colored lights.
Heaven and Hell Stories: Randy Gehling (June 18, 2012) *Heaven and Hell Stories* Retrieved from http://heavenandhellstories.blogspot.com/2012/06/randy-gehlings-near-death-experience.html

[37] David enters into a heavenly city complete with various plants and waterways whose natural beauty surpasses that of Earth. He also notes that the beings there appeared to him without bodies, and the energy they emitted communicated their level of spiritual evolution.
Williams, Kevin. (Sept 16, 2019) "David Oakford's Near-Death Experience" *Near-Death Experiences and the Afterlife*. Retrieved from

https://near-death.com/david-oakford/

[38] Diane also experiences a heavenly city, complete with beautiful buildings and divinely beautiful elements of nature. The beings are energy fields without physical bodies. These beings have "job" roles that tend to be more creative in nature and mirror what they will do in their next physical life. Unlike life on earth, the beings do not experience pain and suffering.

Diane G NDE 175 (n.d.) *NDERF*. Retrieved from https://www.nderf.org/Experiences/1diane_g_nde.html

[39] This anonymous account is a beautiful one. Though the experiencer sees a "river of life", it does not appear in the city itself. The "river" is composed of the composite experiences of all beings, the collective knowledge of all. I placed this river in the heavenly city from the reference to the River of Life in heaven in Revelation 22:1.

"Shimmering River of Life" (April 25, 2015). *International Association for Near-Death Studies, Inc*. Retrieved from https://iands.org/ndes/nde-stories/85-shimmering-river-of-life.html

[40] Philippians 1:6

[41] George Ritchie's is one of the most well-known of NDE experiences. Ritchie experiences two levels of heaven. The first is the Temple of Wisdom, where spirits engage in learning and the arts. The second is for more evolved souls, those who more closely aligned their lives with Jesus' while on Earth.

Williams, Kevin. (2019, September 26). *George Ritchie's Near-Death Experience*. Near-Death Experiences and the Afterlife. Retrieved from https://near-death.com/george-ritchie-nde/

[42] Matthew 5:48

[43] Rev. Storm explains that as we evolve, both on Earth and in the spiritual realm (and potentially in other physical lives) to become more Christlike, there are many opportunities available to us. The goal is union with God, where we become like God while keeping what makes us unique. We become co-creators in creation. Storm explains that we can take roles as guardian angels or shadow other more evolved beings. We have an infinite number of possibilities for our growth and there is no need to hurry the process. Storm is clear that God does not desire us to rush through this process. There is no "urgency or anxiety".

Storm, Howard (2005). *My Descent into Death: A Second Chance at Life*. Doubleday. P 56-58.

[44] Nancy speaks of thin, delicate strands of divine love that connect us with others.

Rynes, Nancy (2015). *Awakenings from the Light: 12 Life Lessons from a Near-Death Experience*. [Kindle Cloud Reader Version]. Retrieved from amazon.com Location No. 1322, 1576.

[45] Like so many others who have an NDE, Dr. Alexander notes multiple times that the experience of time is different on the spiritual plane.
Alexander, Eben, M.D. (2012). *Proof of Heaven: A Neurosurgeon's Journey into the Afterlife*. Simon & Schuster Paperbacks. P 30-31, 69

[46] Nancy recounts her struggle with being sent back. She is fully against returning and her guide shows her pieces of her future, both short and long-term, to help her to muster up the courage to return.
Rynes, Nancy (2015). *Awakenings from the Light: 12 Life Lessons from a Near-Death Experience*. [Kindle Cloud Reader Version]. Retrieved from amazon.com Location No.671-683

Linda is told that she would not be able to remember everything from her experience as that knowledge would interfere with her experience on the physical plane.
Linda G NDE 3649. (n.d.) NDERF. Retrieved from
https://www.nderf.org/Experiences/1linda_g_nde.html

[47] Linda recounts (scroll down to the Q & A section to find this information) that souls have the opportunity to map out the plans for their lives. These plans include our parents, bodies, and general life plans. Most goals are relatively simple in nature rather than "save the world" or "be president". Some goals are as simple as to enjoy playing a sport or to enjoy the food, and experiences that can only be had in the type of physical body that we have here on this planet.
Linda G NDE 3649. (n.d.) NDERF. Retrieved from
https://www.nderf.org/Experiences/1linda_g_nde.html

[48] This is the first mention of the concept of reincarnation in the narrative. Again, I include this in order to be consistent with what I believe is representative of the hundreds of NDE accounts I have read (including Amy's, below). For readers who come from a traditional Christian background and may be uncomfortable with this concept, you may enjoy Diane's explanation of having the opportunity to determine these challenges before birth but having only one life to live. She speaks from a Christian perspective.
Amy C NDE 4720 (n.d.) *NDERF*. Retrieved from:
https://www.nderf.org/Experiences/1amy_c_nde_4720.html
Diane C NDE 321 (n.d.) *NDERF*. Retrieved from:
https://www.nderf.org/Experiences/1diane_c_nde.html

[49] Deborah has a quite extensive NDE-like dream where she speaks to her recently deceased brother. In the experience two scenarios are shown: difficulties based on planned choices and difficulties due to inexperience. Her brother apologizes to Deborah for how his illness might have affected

her, explaining that his living with HIV/AIDS was something he needed to do for himself. He also explains that Deborah needs to let go of her judgment and anger at their cousins, whom he described as "spiritually handicapped". He explained that you wouldn't be angry at a person with no arms for not being able to play catch—the same was true on a spiritual level for the immature and self-seeking behavior of their relatives.

Deborah L. NDE-Like 7961. (n.d.) *NDERF*. Retrieved from https://www.nderf.org/Experiences/1deborah_l_ndelike.html

[50] Anita is clear that there should be no judgment of other souls while on Earth. She reinforces the idea that all souls are interconnected and united. Judgment and fear/competition are products of the mind.

Anita M NDE 2766/11068. (n.d.) *NDERF*. Retrieved from https://www.nderf.org/Experiences/1anita_m_nde.html

[51] Matthew 22:39

[52] Juliet explains that Earth is a hologram created by the collective consciousness for our learning and growth. She explains that the ultimate destiny of every soul is to return to the Light, which is pure love. Earth is just one step along the way, and as a hologram, is still a part of heaven.

Williams, Kevin. (2019, September 18). *Juliet Nightingale's Near-Death Experience.* Near-Death Experiences and the Afterlife. Retrieved from https://near-death.com/juliet-nightingale/

[53] Some goals are as simple as to enjoy playing a sport or to enjoy the food, experiences that can only be had in the type of physical body that we have here on this planet.

Linda G NDE 3649. (n.d.) *NDERF*. Retrieved from https://www.nderf.org/Experiences/1linda_g_nde.html

[54] Visiting other planets is not common among NDEs in general but is prevalent in more extensive experiences. Roger and Sandi's NDEs are the most detailed examples and are the basis for the remainder of this chapter. All pertinent details from the text are backed by these experiences and are well worth the read! Both Roger and Sandi visit other planets with various different beings. Some are more evolved and some less evolved than humans. The most evolved are more in harmony with the planet and are conscious of the spiritual realm. I highly recommend both of these accounts. Other accounts, such as Howard Storm's, mention life on other planets but the experiencer does not visit the planets during the experience.

Sandi T NDEs 9082 (n.d) *NDERF*. Retrieved from https://www.nderf.org/Experiences/1sandi_t_ndes.html

Roger C NDE 744. (n.d.) *NDERF*. Retrieved from https://www.nderf.org/Experiences/1roger_c_nde.html

[55] John 21:1-14

[56] Both Beth and Cara reference meeting with relatives in their NDEs. Cara had never met her grandfather on the physical plane, but he was there to greet her and comfort her during her NDE. Beth is clear that the soul who was her mother in her current life (the mother had died a year prior to Beth's NDE) had been both a spiritual guide on both the spiritual and Earthly planes. When Linda returns from her experience, she is able to see the spirit guides of others, whether angel or another soul acting as a guide. There have been occasions when strangers ask her to describe their guide and the stranger recognizes the description as a deceased loved one.

Cara NDE 3637. (n.d.) *NDERF*. Retrieved from
https://www.nderf.org/Experiences/1cara_nde.html
Beth B NDE 4277. (n.d.) *NDERF*. Retrieved from
https://www.nderf.org/Experiences/1beth_b_nde.html
Linda S Probable NDE. (n.d.) *NDERF*. Retrieved from
https://www.nderf.org/Experiences/1linda_s_probable_nde.html

[57] The story here is largely inspired by Linda's NDE. Prior to her death, she receives guidance from messages delivered through clear voices heard from within. The guidance went counter to the advice of the doctors but was ultimately what saved her newborn's life. When she transitions, Linda recognizes the telepathic voice of her guide as the same as her "conscience". During her life review, she witnesses an angel guiding her through an interaction with a new playmate at school, helping her overcome her fears. She is also shown a scene from her future when she is at a point of despair and multiple angels surround her to bring her comfort.

Linda B NDE 1030/10084/10085 (n.d.) *NDERF*. Retrieved from
https://www.nderf.org/Experiences/1linda_b_nde_1030.html

[58] The narrative for the bulk of this chapter draws heavily from Joe and Rev. Storm's NDEs. Both men's experiences start in a hellish fashion, with being coerced down a hallway and being tortured by what are described as demon-like spirits. Rev. Storm gives a description of the state of his heart at the time, on which I base Jesus' description of Bob. Rev. Storm, as you might imagine, is a very different man now than he was before his experience!

Joe G NDE 1058. (n.d.) *NDERF*. Retrieved from
https://www.nderf.org/Experiences/1joe_g_nde.html
Storm, Howard (2005). *My Descent into Death: A Second Chance at Life*. Doubleday. P 10-18.

[59] Rev. Storm, having experienced both "hell" and "heaven," explains as it is told to him by Jesus what happens when we die. Ultimately, we make the decision on whether or not to accept God, and God respects our decision.

Storm, Howard (2005). *My Descent into Death: A Second Chance at Life*.

Doubleday. P 49-55.

[60] William passed through a tunnel where he saw souls who hung in the shadows because they felt unworthy of being in the light.
William Si NDE 1198. (n.d.) *NDERF*. Retrieved from https://www.nderf.org/Experiences/1william_si_nde.html

[61] George describes angels attempting to "wake" souls who were in a deep soul sleep, waiting for a future event that they believed deeply in that would resurrect them. He also discusses hell and states that the only reason souls stay there is their own choice—they can leave at any time. I remember reading an NDE with angels crying over "hell", but unfortunately cannot locate the source.
Williams, Kevin. (2019, September 26). *George Ritchie's Near-Death Experience*. Near-Death Experiences and the Afterlife. Retrieved from https://near-death.com/george-ritchie-nde/

[62] Luke 15:7

[63] All 3 of the sources listed in prior citations for this chapter (Rev. Storm, George Ritchie and Joe's) explain in great deal the process of a soul being rescued from hell by angels. Demons cannot tolerate speech of God and flee, as they desire to separate themselves as far as possible from God and from love. James' account is more brief but is also clear that calling out to God leads to immediate rescue.
James S NDE 127. (n.d.) *NDERF*.
https://www.nderf.org/Experiences/1james_s_nde.html

[64] Jesus tells Rev. Storm that Jesus has been to every world throughout time and space to bring the truth of God to beings with the intelligence to receive it. More welcomed him gladly than rejected him.
Storm, Howard (2005). *My Descent into Death: A Second Chance at Life*. Doubleday. P 76.

[65] Jesus' full knowledge of the state of Earth—both its beauty and joy as well as ugliness and pain—were clear to Dr. Neal. Jesus took all this in and blessed it with love.
Neal, Mary C. M.D. (2017). *7 Lessons from Heaven: How Dying Taught Me to Live a Joy-Filled Life*. Convergent Books.

[66] Rev. Storm is a great source to read if you struggle with this chapter. He says "No one will go to God except through the atonement of Christ, the love of Christ, and the way of Christ. Jesus' teachings and practice were inclusive of all people." Rev. Storm is clear (p 64 of his book) that at the end of our life, if we love God, we come to him. It is that simple. Loving God does not mean giving lip service to Jesus. It has everything to do with the state of our hearts.
Storm, Howard (2005). *My Descent into Death: A Second Chance at Life*. Doubleday. P 67

[67] The image of a mountain is a common metaphor for the common spiritual aim of the world's many religions. However, the message comes from the revelation given to Rev. Storm in his NDE. Jesus explained that no one comes to heaven except through coming to know the "Divine Activity of God"/the creative power by which everything was created, which is who Jesus is. However, how a person comes to know God takes many forms. Religion is a way to find God and true religion is the love of God in all that a person does. How an individual chooses to develop in the religion they are a part of is far more important than the choice of a specific faith tradition itself.

Storm, Howard (2005). *My Descent into Death: A Second Chance at Life*. Doubleday. P 55, 73.

[68] Dr. Alexander's NDE included the blessing of moving into and out of the core several times, witnessing orbs going to and from a central source of light. The orbs varied in appearance based on stage of development and entered/exited the source as was needed to fulfill their purposes. James' experience of the light/the core was similar.

Alexander, Eben M.D. (2012). *Proof of Heaven: A Neurosurgeon's Journey into the Afterlife*. Simon & Schuster Paperbacks. P 45-49.
James T NDE 10080. (n.d.) NDERF. Retrieved from
https://www.nderf.org/Experiences/1james_t_nde.html

[69] Dr. Alexander is told that the singing is an irresistible urge/instinct of the souls. Their joy is so overpowering that it overflows in song. Dr. Alexander's is the most memorable of the accounts, but others mention music/singing and explain that it is an outpouring of gratitude and love back to God.

Alexander, Eben M.D. (2012). *Proof of Heaven: A Neurosurgeon's Journey into the Afterlife*. Simon & Schuster Paperbacks. P 45.

[70] What follows draws heavily from Roger and David's NDEs. Both Roger and David rose through the "core", experiencing higher and higher levels of the essence of God. Roger describes 3 levels of the light: love, knowledge, and creation. David realizes that his physical body faded as he rose through the levels of heaven. The glory was overwhelming to the point that he could not handle the intensity and retreated back "down". David also speaks of creation occurring at the highest level of the "core".

Roger C NDE 744. (n.d.) *NDERF*. Retrieved from
https://www.nderf.org/Experiences/1roger_c_nde.html
David NDE 24. (n.d.) *NDERF*. Retrieved from
https://www.nderf.org/Experiences/1david_nde.html

[71] As a math teacher, how could I leave this out? Both Amy and Marie's NDEs reference understanding the beauty of the math and science underlying all of creation.

Amy C NDE 4720. (n.d.) *NDERF.* Retrieved from https://www.nderf.org/Experiences/1amy_c_nde_4720.html
Marie E NDE 813. (n.d.) *NDERF.* Retrieved from https://www.nderf.org/Experiences/1marie_e_nde.html
[72] The response of Jesus stated here is taken directly from Cathleen's experience. I found it the most simplistic and yet beautiful. The response given to Sandi from her guide is more complex and worth the read.
Cathleen C NDE 3735. (n.d.) *NDERF.* Retrieved from https://www.nderf.org/Experiences/1cathleen_c_nde.html
Sandi T NDEs 9082. (n.d.) *NDERF.* Retrieved from https://www.nderf.org/Experiences/1sandi_t_ndes.html
[73] Dr. Alexander explains that a higher amount of contrast is present on our planet than on others.
Alexander, Eben M.D. (2012). *Proof of Heaven: A Neurosurgeon's Journey into the Afterlife.* Simon & Schuster Paperbacks. P 83.
[74] Juliet explains that the Earth is created by the collective consciousness for the purpose of growth and evolution of souls. She describes Earth as a hologram.
Juliet N NDE 10077. (n.d.) *NDERF.* Retrieved from https://www.nderf.org/Experiences/1juliet_n_nde.html
[75] In many NDEs (especially shorter ones), the experiencer is not given a choice. They are simply told it is not their time and they return to their bodies. However, for those with longer experiences (as far as time is relevant in heaven), there does appear to be a choice given. Usually the guide, whether Jesus, a relative, or another spiritual being strongly advises one way or the other. In Jennifer's case, she was adamantly against going back and argued intensely with Jesus about the return. She was shown the car accident scene and understood that she was needed to save the driver of the car, asked to go back to help her mother, and finally convinced to return out of sheer love for Christ. Nevie's case was different—she was told she could not return, that her body was too broken. Nevie expressed faith that God could and would heal her body and explained that she did not want to be reborn and experience childhood again. Nevie was granted the ability to return.
Jennifer V NDE 3318. (n.d.) *NDERF.* Retrieved from https://www.nderf.org/Experiences/1jennifer_v_nde.html
Nevie G NDE 2283. (n.d.) *NDERF.* Retrieved from https://www.nderf.org/Experiences/1nevie_g_nde.html
[76] Amy experiences the many prayers being said for her while in a tunnel at the start of her experience. She can reach out and touch as well as hear these prayers. Nilda saw prayers as points of light on the Earth.
Amy C NDE 8529. (n.d.) *NDERF.* Retrieved from

https://www.nderf.org/Experiences/1amy_c_nde_8259.html
Nilda P NDE 5123. (n.d.) *NDERF*. Retrieved from
https://www.nderf.org/Experiences/1nilda_p_nde.html

[77] Ned Dougherty is told by an angel/light being that prayer groups are the way to avoid the very tumultuous transformation of the Earth through human violence and natural disaster. The being shared that prayers of a group of about twenty strong could save an entire nation from war. Prayer (and meditation as a way to hear God's response) is clearly explained to be the way to fully understand and participate in God's plan for the world.

Williams, Kevin. (2019, September 18). *Ned Dougherty's Near-Death Experience*. Near-Death Experiences and the Afterlife. Retrieved from https://near-death.com/ned-dougherty/

[78] In her NDE, Mary is told that one of her sons will pass on as a young adult. Mary spends the intervening years struggling with this knowledge. Bobby has two NDEs as a young child (2 years and 4 years old). In the second, he is told that he will experience more pain after returning as a result of remembering too much from his NDE. He explains both what he saw in his NDE and how it affected him knowing certain elements of his future. It does seem that the deeper/longer the NDE and the more of them individuals have, the more they remember.

Neal, Mary C. M.D. (2017). *7 Lessons from Heaven: How Dying Taught Me to Live a Joy-Filled Life*. Convergent Books.
Bobby R NDE 8010. (n.d.). *NDERF*. Retrieved from
https://www.nderf.org/Experiences/1bobby_r_nde.html

[79] Linda's experience summarizes well what is remembered and what is not from an experience. Linda is also another example of someone who may have changed the guide's decision—she chooses to come back for her children. She remembers visiting various levels of heaven but can only recall details of the first couple. She also retains the memory of asking God many questions and receiving many answers. However, she can recall very little of the conversation. She is told by her guide that she would need to forget most of what she experienced so that it would not interfere with her life, specifically that remembering too much would rob her life of joy.

Linda G NDE 3649. (n.d.) *NDERF*. Retrieved from
https://www.nderf.org/Experiences/1linda_g_nde.html

[80] Nancy experiences and is taught that love flows through everything in existence.

Rynes, Nancy (2015). *Awakenings from the Light: 12 Life Lessons from a Near-Death Experience*. [Kindle Cloud Reader Version]. Retrieved from amazon.com Location No. 826

[81] Nancy explains that Earth is love expressed on the physical plane.
Rynes, Nancy (2015). *Awakenings from the Light: 12 Life Lessons from a*

Near-Death Experience. [Kindle Cloud Reader Version]. Retrieved from amazon.com Location No. 1298

[82] This metaphor of the stars comes directly from Dr. Alexander. He also explains well the nature of the mind as a filter and methods for training our mind—for working with it to connect more easily to the truth of who we are/to heaven. Most of the rest of the chapter is sourced from his NDE. Alexander, Eben Dr. *Proof of Heaven: A Neurosurgeon's Journey into the Afterlife*. Simon & Schuster Paperbacks. P 72, 80-86.

[83] Another wonderful NDE that explains how the mind is a filter is Dr. Bell's. This is one of the few Eastern NDEs I encountered (from Hong Kong). However, the experience is very similar to the western NDEs I have read.

Dr. Bell C NDE. (n.d.) *NDERF*. Retrieved from https://www.nderf.org/Experiences/1bell_c_nde.html

[84] Rev. Storm explains the value of being trusted by God to step away from the spiritual plane/leave home and have free will, much like an adolescent would.

Storm, Howard (2005). *My Descent into Death: A Second Chance at Life*. Doubleday. P 62-63.

[85] Nancy explains that if we ignore the spiritual guidance given to us, that voice gradually weakens.

Rynes, Nancy (2015). *Awakenings from the Light: 12 Life Lessons from a Near-Death Experience*. [Kindle Cloud Reader Version]. Retrieved from amazon.com Location No. 1716

[86] Matthew 26:41

[87] Jesus tells Rev. Storm to "Be very still and allow God to love you. You will feel the love around you and inside you."

Storm, Howard. (2005). *My Descent into Death: A Second Chance at Life*. Doubleday. P 83.

[88] John 14:12

[89] Mark 1:35

[90] Luke 10:42

[91] Joshua 10

[92] Glauco had a simultaneous NDE with two of her brothers. All three children confirmed that they were saved from drowning by an angel though they did not experience each other's presence during the NDE itself. Glauco says that from her NDE, she understands that the Bible is our guidebook to get back home and is all about the love that she felt in her experience.

Glauco S NDE 3674. (n.d.) *NDERF*. Retrieved from https://www.nderf.org/Experiences/1glauco_s_nde.html

[93] William had three NDEs. In his last NDE, Jesus told William to take

one of the principles that Jesus taught and work with it until it becomes "second nature," then move to another.
William Si NDE 119. (n.d.) *NDERF*. Retrieved from https://www.nderf.org/Experiences/1william_si_nde.html

[94] Matthew 6:25-34

[95] Matthew 5:21-26

[96] Jesus tells Rev. Storm that God has sent a large number of teachers to the Earth.
Storm, Howard. (2005). *My Descent into Death: A Second Chance at Life.* Doubleday. P 78.

[97] Rev. Storm, in his argument with Jesus, claims that he cannot return since the world is filled primarily with ugliness and evil. Jesus agrees that the ugliness and evil exist, but explains that there is more than enough love, goodness and beauty for those who seek it. He goes on to say that people will find in the world what they have within them and what they look for.

Anita explains that even our physical health depends on our inner energy. She explains that long-term illnesses such as cancer begin as a spiritual sickness. Anita herself was healed from lymphoma as a result of her experience. Anita also echoes Rev. Storm and explains that what we choose to see in the world is what we will find. She recommends focusing on loving yourself unconditionally, as the way we see ourselves affects how we see the world around us.
Storm, Howard (2005). *My Descent into Death: A Second Chance at Life.* Doubleday. P 77.
Anita M NDE 2766/11068. (n.d.) *NDERF*. Retrieved from https://www.nderf.org/Experiences/1anita_m_nde.html

[98] Nancy experiences colors in her surroundings vibrating with joy and the peace, love and joy seem to intensify the colors themselves.
Rynes, Nancy (2015). *Awakenings from the Light: 12 Life Lessons from a Near-Death Experience.* [Kindle Cloud Reader Version]. Retrieved from amazon.com Location No. 491-503.

[99] The image of ripples on a pond is taken directly from Rynes' NDE retelling. The concept that our actions affect others is pervasive in many accounts, but this powerful image was the best I had read to illustrate the concept. This is a great work and I highly recommend the book to any interested in reading further on the topic.
Rynes, Nancy (2015). *Awakenings from the Light: 12 Life Lessons from a Near-Death Experience.* [Kindle Cloud Reader Version]. Retrieved from amazon.com Location No.2373-2452

[100] Matthew 13:44

[101] This is taken from what is my favorite moment in any NDE experience. Rev. Storm is arguing with Jesus about going back (he is very

against it) and claims that the world will go on quite well without him. Jesus tells him that he can save the world. When asked how, Jesus responds "You are to love the person you are with." Jesus explains that love spreads quickly from one to another—the strongest force and the only way to transform Earth. Jesus says that Rev. Storm will not be alone and that there are millions of people in on this plan.

Storm, Howard (2005). *My Descent into Death: A Second Chance at Life*. Doubleday. P 82

[102] Anita recommends working to love yourself unconditionally. She explains that the way you see yourself strongly impacts how you see the world.

Anita M NDE 2766/11068. (n.d.) *NDERF*. Retrieved from https://www.nderf.org/Experiences/1anita_m_nde.html

[103] Anita explains the difference between being loving and being love. In being love, you love yourself so much that the love overflows, spilling from your being. Anita describes this as being a vessel that love flows through. She explains that because the love comes from within, it is not dependent on others' behavior.

Anita M NDE 2766/11068. (n.d.) *NDERF*. Retrieved from https://www.nderf.org/Experiences/1anita_m_nde.html

[104] One of Barbara's main take-aways from her childhood NDE experience was God's urging to love others as we love God, as all souls are a part of the creator. She beautifully contrasts humanity's worldly concept of love with the love we are called to have for each other.

Barbara S NDE 7375/5023/2102. (n.d.) *NDERF*. Retrieved from https://www.nderf.org/Experiences/1barbara_s_nde.html

[105] Luke 23:34

[106] Nancy explains that other souls can be mirrors, messengers and teachers.

Rynes, Nancy (2015). *Awakenings from the Light: 12 Life Lessons from a Near-Death Experience*. [Kindle Cloud Reader Version]. Retrieved from amazon.com Location No. 1197

[107] Matthew 7:3

[108] Rev. Storm expresses doubt on whether the plan of loving the person before you will work to save the world. Jesus responds, "This is God's will, and it will be done." Jesus also explains the chain reaction effect of love—each person reaching out to others, and them reaching out to even more, etc.

Storm, Howard (2005). *My Descent into Death: A Second Chance at Life*. Doubleday. P 82

[109] Many NDEs that are exceptional in nature have visions of the future. A few of these predictions have already taken place. Interestingly, 9/11 was

seen in a few of the NDEs. The consensus among almost all, including the three cited below, is that the relatively near future will have a time of war as well as large-scale natural disasters. A few mention that the natural disasters are caused by the altering of the Earth's tilt by an asteroid or something similar.

Lou F NDE 2422/70. (n.d.) *NDERF*. Retrieved from https://www.nderf.org/Experiences/1lou_f_nde.html
Rick R NDE 24. (n.d.) *NDERF*. Retrieved from https://www.nderf.org/Experiences/1rick_r_nde.html
Williams, Kevin. (2019, September 18). *Ned Dougherty's Near-Death Experience*. Near-Death Experiences and the Afterlife. Retrieved from https://near-death.com/ned-dougherty/

[110] In Rev. Storm's NDE, Jesus and the angels explain that wars are a result of humanity's collective desire for domination, often masked by nationalism. They also explain that the transition from the current state of the world to the future idyllic state will take place within about 200 years.

Storm, Howard (2005). *My Descent into Death: A Second Chance at Life*. Doubleday. P 40-44

[111] Following these extreme events, Earth becomes the home to a more highly evolved humanity who live in harmony with nature and each other. Rev. Storm is shown this new idyllic life in great detail. Thus, most of the discussion that follows of these new communities on Earth derives from his account. There are other accounts that show a similar idyllic Earth, but Rev. Storm's account is the most detailed that I have read.

Storm, Howard (2005). *My Descent into Death: A Second Chance at Life*. Doubleday. P 44-48

[112] Mark 11: 22-23

[113] Jesus tells Rev. Storm that scientific discoveries are God-inspired. He reveals the discoveries that will come in the future, when humanity is ready for such knowledge: telepathy, travel through space and time, knowledge through contemplation, and controlling physical objects' energy with our minds.

Storm, Howard (2005). *My Descent into Death: A Second Chance at Life*. Doubleday. P 43-44

[114] All four articles are interesting. The study on prayer gives examples of research that both supports and counters the benefits of prayer on healing. When we keep in mind that some medical outcomes are part of the plans of our lives, we must understand that when a prayer does not have the outcome we expect, it does not mean the prayer has failed. What is more important is the state of our connection to the divine, which prayer helps in both the one praying and the one prayed for.

Solanki, Hitesh A. (2015). The Effect of Music on Physico-Chemical

Parameters of Selected Plants. *International Journal of Plant, Animal, and Environmental Sciences.*5(1).
Andrade C, Radhakrishnan R. Prayer and healing: A medical and scientific perspective on randomized controlled trials. *Indian J Psychiatry.* 2009;51(4):247-253. doi:10.4103/0019-5545.58288
Elmholdt, E. M., Skewes, J., Dietz, M., Møller, A., Jensen, M. S., Roepstorff, A., Wiech, K., & Jensen, T. S. (2017). Reduced Pain Sensation and Reduced BOLD Signal in Parietofrontal Networks during Religious Prayer. *Frontiers in human neuroscience, 11*, 337. https://doi.org/10.3389/fnhum.2017.00337
Serpell J. (1991). Beneficial effects of pet ownership on some aspects of human health and behaviour. *Journal of the Royal Society of Medicine, 84*(12), 717–720.

[115] Jennifer's guide takes her to the scene of the accident to rouse her compassion and help ease her back into her Earthly body.
Jennifer V NDE 3318. (n.d.) *NDERF.* Retrieved from https://www.nderf.org/Experiences/1jennifer_v_nde.html

[116] Dr. Neal explains that angels intervene whenever they are needed. They may suddenly appear and fade. Angels look and act like humans on the Earthly plane, though they are typically on the tall side (close to 7 feet).

A number of experiencers had miraculous recoveries. Aislinn's is quite normal. Especially in the case of long NDE's, where the experiencer is clinically dead for a significant portion of time, the physical level of healing is usually extreme. Nancy's guide, right before Nancy returns to her body, puts her hands on the broken places from her car accident to heal them, much like the angels in Aislinn's story heal Aislinn's damaged lungs.

Neal, Mary C. M.D. (2017). *7 Lessons from Heaven: How Dying Taught Me to Live a Joy-Filled Life.* Convergent Books.
Rynes, Nancy (2015). *Awakenings from the Light: 12 Life Lessons from a Near-Death Experience.* [Kindle Cloud Reader Version]. Retrieved from amazon.com Location No.683-694.

[117] Dr. Neal explains that more than half of all married NDE experiencers end up getting a divorce following their experience. The spouse often struggles to believe the experiencer and/or is very unsettled by the changes in them.

Neal, Mary C. M.D. (2017). *7 Lessons from Heaven: How Dying Taught Me to Live a Joy-Filled Life.* Convergent Books.

[118] Submersion for longer than 10 minutes decreases survival (12% or less survival). Brain and lung damage are likely.

Parenteau, Michael, MC, USN., Stockinger Zsolt, MC, USN, et al. (2018, September 5). Drowning Management. *Military Medicine, 183*(2). pages 172-179. https://doi.org/10.1093/milmed/usy136

[119] Like many experiencers, Linda struggled in her re-adjustment to the Earthly plain. Her transition was made more difficult due to her extended illness. Linda struggled with anger and depression regarding her return for about a year following. However, she also had the ability to see the spirits/guardian angels around others and a glow around objects.

Linda S Probable NDE. (n.d.) *NDERF*. Retrieved from https://www.nderf.org/Experiences/1linda_s_probable_nde.html

[120] Experiencers tend to be able to live more in the present moment, but this may come across as being aloof to others.

Atwater, P.M.H., L.H.D. (2017, December 14). *Aftereffects of Near-Death States*. IANDS.

Retrieved from https://iands.org/aftereffects-of-near-death-states.html

[121] Experiencers tend to live more in the present moment, have a more philosophical approach to life, be more relaxed/less driven and more forgiving. They communicate differently and may struggle with bouts of depression as they adjust to what is now a foreign landscape. One of the stranger "after-effects" of having an NDE is electrical sensitivity. Watches, microphones, televisions, radios, and even streetlights stop working or malfunction.

Atwater, P.M.H., L.H.D. (2017, December 14). *Aftereffects of Near-Death States*. IANDS.

Retrieved from https://iands.org/aftereffects-of-near-death-states.html

[122] Experiencers tend to have a more universal love for all people. This causes them to be generous with many people but more detached in intimate relationships. This is one of the causes of the high rate of divorce among experiencers as the spouse feels that they are no longer "special". However, in truth, the experiencer loves all more genuinely.

Atwater, P.M.H., L.H.D. (2017, December 14). *Aftereffects of Near-Death States*. IANDS.

Retrieved from https://iands.org/aftereffects-of-near-death-states.html

[123] Being able to intuitively feel the deeper emotions and hidden thoughts of others—seeing behind the facade—is common among experiencers.

Atwater, P.M.H., L.H.D. (2017, December 14). *Aftereffects of Near-Death States*. IANDS.

Retrieved from https://iands.org/aftereffects-of-near-death-states.html

[124] Mark 9:24, NKJV

[125] The experience Dave has in the church is my own. When my grandfather (Pop in this story) passed and I prayed for his help in taking care of our mourning extended family, he came to me in an experience much like this one. It is the closest I have ever come to having an NDE, and, though a small experience, it was life-altering in nature. For those

curious, the character of "Pop" is almost entirely taken from my grandfather, even down to the dialogue. All other characters are fictional in nature, though Aislinn and Dave share some characteristics with my husband and myself.

[126] Telepathy, visions of the future, and awareness of the presence of spiritual beings are all common for experiencers.

Atwater, P.M.H., L.H.D. (2017, December 14). *Aftereffects of Near-Death States*. IANDS. Retrieved from https://iands.org/aftereffects-of-near-death-states.html

[127] The ability to perform physical healing has been reported after returning from an NDE experience.

Atwater, P.M.H., L.H.D. (2017, December 14). *Aftereffects of Near-Death States*. IANDS. Retrieved from https://iands.org/aftereffects-of-near-death-states.html

Made in the USA
Middletown, DE
13 November 2022